ACKNOWLEDGEMENT

My thanks are due to Fiat for their unstinted co-operation and also for supplying data and illustrations.

Considerable assistance has also been given by owners, who have discussed their cars in detail, and I would like to express my gratitude for this invaluable advice and help.

Kenneth Ball
Associate Member, Guild of Motoring Writers
Ditchling Sussex England.

This book is to be returned on or before the last date stamped below.

STORE

Michael McLarens, Executive Director, Autobooks Ltd, with his Fiat X1/9 at 5000 miles

Fiat X1/9 1974-77 Autobook

By Kenneth Ball

Associate Member, Guild of Motoring Writers
and the Autobooks Team of Technical Writers

Fiat X1/9 1974-77

Autobooks Ltd. Golden Lane Brighton BN1 2QJ England

The AUTOBOOK series of Workshop Manuals is the largest in the world and covers the majority of British and Continental motor cars, as well as the majority of Japanese and Australian models.

Whilst every care has been taken to ensure correctness of information it is obviously not possible to guarantee complete freedom from errors or omissions or to accept liability arising from such errors or omissions.

CONTENTS

ISBN 0 85147 721 6

First Edition   1978

© Autobooks Ltd 1978

928

Printed in Brighton England for Autobooks Ltd by G. Beard and Son Ltd
Bound in Hove England for Autobooks Ltd by Jilks Ltd

A

INTRODUCTION

This do-it-yourself Workshop Manual has been specially written for the owner who wishes to maintain his vehicle in first class condition and to carry out the bulk of his own servicing and repairs. Considerable savings on garage charges can be made, and one can drive in safety and confidence knowing the work has been done properly.

Comprehensive step-by-step instructions and illustrations are given on most dismantling, overhauling and assembling operations. Certain assemblies require the use of expensive special tools, the purchase of which would be unjustified. In these cases information is included but the reader is recommended to hand the unit to the agent for attention.

Throughout the Manual hints and tips are included which will be found invaluable, and there is an easy to follow fault diagnosis at the end of each chapter.

Whilst every care has been taken to ensure correctness of information it is obviously not possible to guarantee complete freedom from errors or omissions or to accept liability arising from such errors or omissions.

Instructions may refer to the righthand or lefthand sides of the vehicle or the components. These are the same as the righthand or lefthand of an observer standing behind the vehicle and looking forward.

CHAPTER 1

THE ENGINE

1:1 Description

The engine is an in-line four cylinder unit, transversely mounted ahead of the rear wheels, and drives the rear wheels through an integrally mounted transmission assembly and two universally-jointed drive shafts. A single overhead camshaft is provided, driven by a synthetic rubber toothed belt with steel cable reinforcement, drive being taken from the crankshaft. This belt also drives the engine auxiliary shaft which operates the oil pump and fuel pump and, on later models, the distributor. On early models, the distributor is horizontally mounted at the end of the cylinder head and is driven directly by the camshaft. A similar type of toothed belt is used to drive the air pump for the emission control system, on models so equipped. Sectional views of the engine assembly are shown in **FIGS 1:1** and **1:2**.

The cast iron cylinder block is integral with the upper half of the crankcase, the lower half of which is formed by the sump. The cylinder head is of light alloy and consists of a lower section attached to the cylinder block, which carries the valve gear and sparking plugs, and an upper section attached to this which carries the camshaft in five plain bearings.

The cast steel crankshaft has integral balance weights and is provided with five plain shell bearings, all of which are pressure lubricated. Axial thrust is accommodated by the main bearing nearest to the flywheel. Similar type shell bearings are fitted to the connecting rods, which have straightcut big-end caps.

The light alloy pistons are of the auto-thermal type, having integrally cast steel retaining rings and full skirts. Two compression rings and one oil control ring are fitted to each piston. Gudgeon pins are a free-fit in the pistons and a press-fit in the connecting rod small-ends.

The gear type oil pump, driven by the engine auxiliary shaft, is located in the lower part of the crankcase. Pressure oil is fully filtered before being passed to the lubrication points in the engine. The external oil filter is of the fullflow type and its mounting incorporates a relief valve which operates to return excess oil to the sump in the event of oil pressure rising higher than the safe maximum.

1:2 Removing and refitting the engine

The normal operations of decarbonising and servicing the cylinder head can be carried out without the need for engine removal, as can the majority of engine servicing

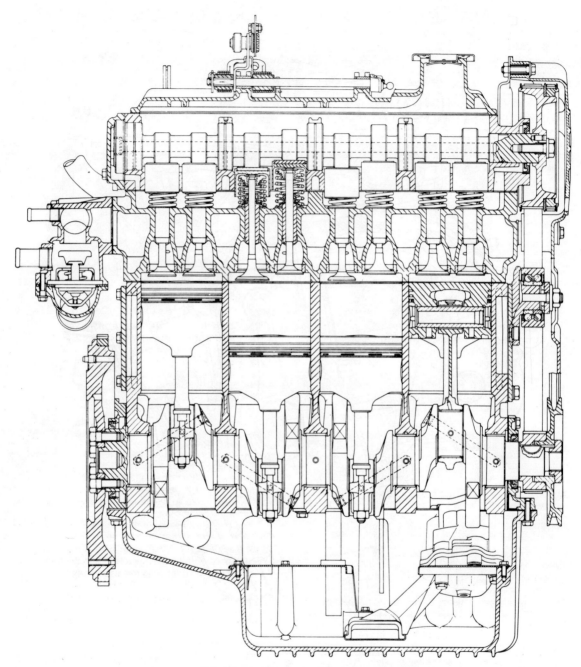

FIG 1:1   Engine longitudinal section

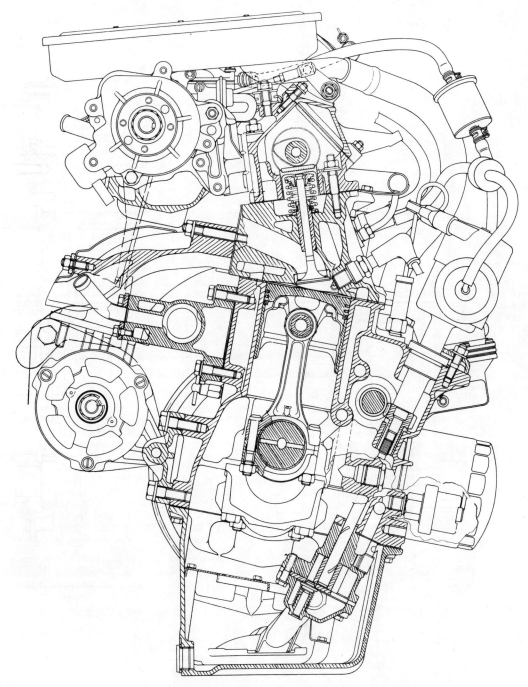

FIG 1:2 Engine cross section, later type with emission control equipment

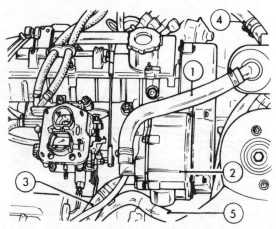

FIG 1:3 Disconnecting air pump and heater hoses

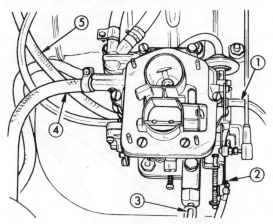

FIG 1:4 Disconnecting carburetter controls

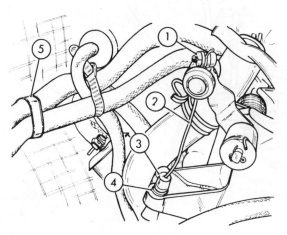

FIG 1:5 Disconnecting fuel hoses and accelerator cable

procedures, including the removal of piston and connecting rod assemblies. However, if crankshaft removal is necessary or attention to the cylinder bores is required, engine removal will be necessary. For some overhaul work, certain special tools are essential and the owner would be well advised to check on the availability of these factory tools or suitable substitutes before tackling the items involved, If the operator is not a skilled automobile engineer, it is suggested that much useful information will be found in **Hints on Maintenance and Overhaul** at the end of this manual and that it be read before starting work.

Owners of vehicles fitted with air conditioning (refrigeration) systems should consult a Fiat service station before attempting engine removal procedures, or any servicing procedure which involves the disconnection or removal of system components or hoses, so that advice can be obtained concerning the discharging of the system. If the pressurised system is opened, liquid refrigerant will escape, immediately evaporating and instantly freezing anything it contacts. Uncontrolled release of refrigerant will cause severe frostbite or possibly more serious injury if it contacts any part of the body. For this reason, all work involving air conditioning system components should be entrusted only to a Fiat service station having the necessary special equipment and trained personnel.

Removal:

Open the front luggage compartment and disconnect the battery cables. On models with fuel evaporative emission control systems (see **Chapter 2**), loosen the fuel filler cap so that atmospheric pressure will be maintained in the fuel tank.

Refer to **Chapter 4** and drain the cooling system, then remove the cap from the expansion tank. Refer to **Chapter 2** and remove the air cleaner assembly.

Refer to **FIG 1:3**. On models with emission control system, disconnect hose 1 between air pump 2 and filter, then disconnect hose 3 from air pump. Separate heater return hose 5 at coupling joint 4, then disconnect heater hose from water pump connection. Disconnect wiring from the alternator. Remove the two bolts securing louvred protection panel at engine compartment rear bulkhead, this being below the activated carbon canister on models with emission control system.

Refer to **FIG 1:4**. Disconnect choke linkage 2 and hoses 1 and 5 from carburetter. Disconnect wires 3 and vent hose 4. Disconnect the wires from the coil at their connections at the distributor, disconnect wires from oil pressure and water temperature sender units and disconnect wiring at starter motor.

Refer to **FIG 1:5**. Remove clamp 5 securing fuel hoses to bulkhead, then disconnect fuel feed and return hoses from bulkhead. Remove bolt 1 from accelerator cable 2, then slide seal 3 from cable. Remove retaining clip 4 from cable sheath. Remove cable from support. Remove bolts securing expansion tank at top and bottom then lift tank and allow coolant to drain into the engine. Disconnect hoses from tank at thermostat housing, then remove tank and hoses. Disconnect remaining cooling system hoses at engine connections.

Refer to **Chapter 5** and remove the clutch slave cylinder without disconnecting the hose, then support cylinder by wiring in engine compartment so that the hose is not strained.

Raise the rear of the car and support safely on floor stands for access to the underside. Remove the rear wheels. Remove the remaining bolt securing louvred panel at rear bulkhead, then remove the panel. Refer to **FIG 1 : 6**. Remove alternator heat shield 2 then remove three panels 3 from bottom of engine compartment. Remove panels 1 located inboard of each rear wheel.

Refer to **Chapter 6** and drain the transmission oil. If the engine is to be dismantled after removal, remove the sump drain plug and allow the oil to drain fully into a suitable container. Refit drain plugs after oil has drained. Disconnect the connectors for reversing lights and, if fitted, seat belt interlock system. Remove clamps as necessary to allow the wires to come free as the engine is removed. Loosen the knurled nut securing speedometer cable at transmission, then remove the cable and position away from the work area. Refer to **Chapter 6** and disconnect gearchange linkage at transmission end. Be sure to mark the connector before removing the fixing bolts then slacken the single bolt at the flexible coupling so that the coupling can be swung clear of the work area.

Refer to **FIG 1 : 7**. Remove the bolt securing earth strap 6 at body connection. Straighten tab washers at exhaust manifold flange, then remove the four nuts and tab washers. Remove the two bolts 1 at upper bracket at lefthand side of silencer 2. Remove two nuts securing

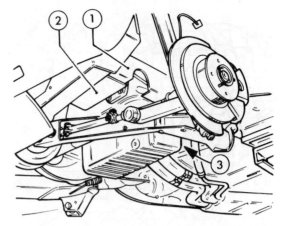

FIG 1 : 6   Removing panels and heat shield

silencer centre support 3 to crossmember, then remove silencer and pipe assembly. Remove two nuts and bolts retaining upper bracket 4 to differential, then remove the bracket. Remove the three bolts securing drive shaft retaining ring 5 on lefthand side, then remove the similar bolts on the righthand side. Slide the boots away from the transmission, allowing the excess oil to drain into a suitable container. Take care to avoid accidental injury on the sharp edges of sheet metal components.

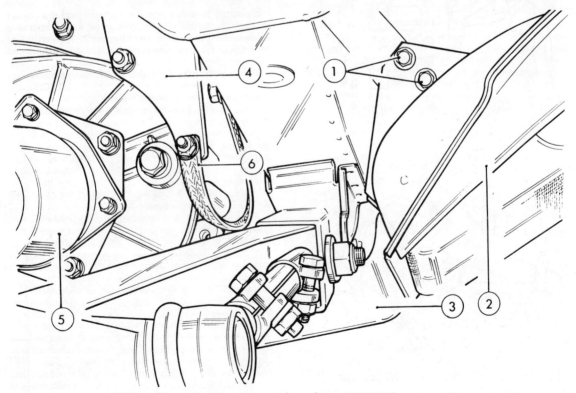

FIG 1 : 7   Disconnecting components in engine compartment

FIG 1:8   Disconnecting components in engine compartment

Refer to **FIG 1:8**. Remove the nut securing handbrake cable bracket 7 at the forward end of each control arm 3. Check and record the number of shims 4 at each control arm mounting point. Remove the four bolts 6, nuts and shims 4 securing control arms 3 to body, then swing the arms downwards out of their brackets 5. Move control arms away from transmission until drive shafts are free from differential, then support drive shafts to avoid strain by wiring to the control arms. Alternatively, the drive shafts

and suspension units can be completely removed for better access, as described in **Chapter 8**. Straighten the lockwashers on two bolts 2 at each end of lower crossmember 1, then loosen but do not remove the bolts.

The engine must now be supported by using a suitable trolley jack with adaptor beneath the sump and transmission, or by lowering the rear of the car until the engine weight is supported on suitable blocks of wood placed on the ground. This done, refer to **FIG 1:9** and, from above

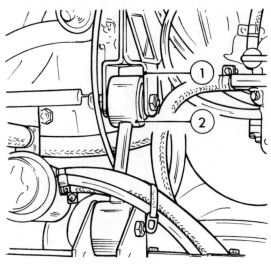

FIG 1:9   Bracket 1 and reaction rod 2

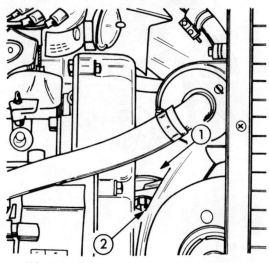

FIG 1:10   Front engine mounting 1 and bolt 2

the engine, disconnect reaction rod 2 from bracket 1 on engine. Refer to **FIG 1:10** and remove bolt 2 from front engine mounting 1. Raise the rear of the car slightly, or lower the engine slightly, as appropriate, then rock the engine and transmission assembly carefully to clear front engine mounting 1. Now carefully raise the rear of the car, or lower the engine on the trolley jack, as appropriate, until the engine and transmission can be removed from beneath the rear of the car.

Refitting:

This is a reversal of the removal procedure, making sure that all component fixings are tightened to the specified torque figures. Use new tab washers, lockwashers and self-locking nuts throughout. Note that rear suspension components should be finally tightened with the car correctly laden, as described in **Chapter 8**.

1:3 Dismantling the engine

Remove the engine as described in **Section 1:2** and clean as much as possible of the dirt and oil from the engine exterior before proceeding, to prevent contamination of the internal components during dismantling. The use of an engine stand is recommended, if available. Alternatively, use suitable blocks of wood to support the engine in the appropriate attitudes for dismantling.

Refer to **Chapter 6** and separate the transmission from the engine. Drain the engine oil, if not done previously. Remove the timing belt as described in **Section 1:5**, then remove the belt tensioner. On models with emission control systems, remove the air pump.

Remove the oil filter, fuel pump and water pump. Remove the distributor as described in **Chapter 3**. Refer to **Section 1:8** and remove the cylinder head. Invert the

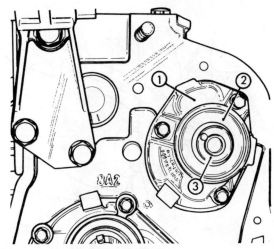

FIG 1:11 Auxiliary shaft flange and seal

engine so that it is standing on the cylinder head joint face, taking care to prevent damage, then remove the oil pump (see **Section 1:12**).

Remove the drive belt pulley from the crankshaft, then the toothed pulley, collecting the key from the shaft. Bend back the locking tab and remove the fixing bolt, then remove the toothed pulley from the auxiliary shaft. Refer to **FIG 1:11** and remove flange 1 and seal 2 from auxiliary shaft 3. Remove the pinion which drives the oil pump, then remove the auxiliary shaft. If the auxiliary shaft bearings are worn or damaged, they must be renewed by a service station having special equipment.

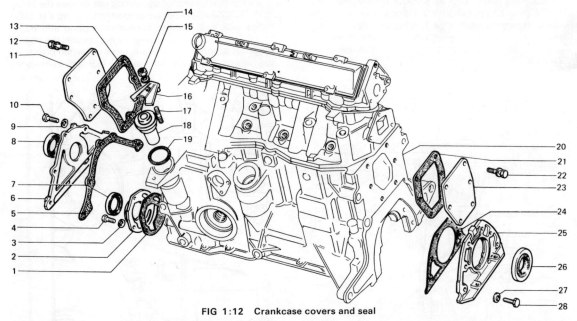

FIG 1:12 Crankcase covers and seal

Key to Fig 1:12 1 Gasket 2 Cover 3 Washer 4 Bolt 5 Gasket 6 Cover 7 Seal 8 Seal 9 Washer 10 Bolt 11 Cover 12 Bolt and washer 13 Gasket 14 Nut 15 Washer 16 Bracket 17 Stud 18 Cover 19 Gasket 20 Crankcase 21 Gasket 22 Bolt and washer 23 Cover 24 Gasket 25 Cover 26 Seal 27 Washer 28 Bolt

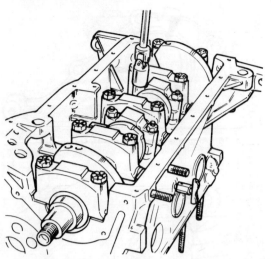

FIG 1:13 Removing main and big-end bearing caps

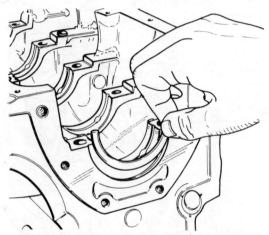

FIG 1:14 Removing crankshaft thrust washers

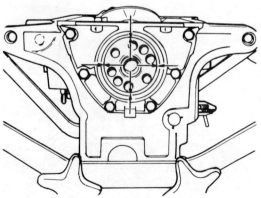

FIG 1:15 Aligning crankcase cover, flywheel side

Mark the position of the flywheel in relation to the crankshaft, so that the original balance of the assembly can be regained when the flywheel is refitted. Lock the flywheel against rotation by suitable means, then remove the fixing bolts and lift off the flywheel.

Remove the covers, seals and gaskets from each end of the crankcase, as shown in **FIG 1:12**. Remove the big-end caps as shown in **FIG 1:13**, keeping caps and bearing shells in the correct order for refitting in their original positions if not to be renewed. Carefully scrape away any carbon ridges found at the tops of the cylinder bores, then remove the piston and connecting rod assemblies, again keeping the components in the correct order. Remove the main bearing caps as shown in **FIG 1:13**, then collect the crankshaft thrust washers from the main bearing position nearest to the flywheel, as shown in **FIG 1:14**, keeping parts in the correct order if not to be renewed. Remove the crankshaft and collect the upper main bearing shells, noting their positions.

Reassembly:

Reassembly of the engine is a reversal of the dismantling procedure, after servicing the components according to the instructions in the appropriate sections of this chapter. Renew all oil seals and gaskets and use new tab washers, lockwashers and self-locking nuts. During reassembly, all moving parts should be coated with engine oil, paying particular attention to main and big-end bearings and to the pistons and cylinder bores.

When refitting crankcase end covers, make sure that the flywheel end cover is centralised as indicated by the arrows in **FIG 1:15** and use the tabs arrowed in **FIG 1:16** to centralise the timing side cover, before tightening down.

1:4 Cylinder block

Thoroughly clean the cylinder block and examine for cracks or other damage, particularly to the machined joint faces. Check the condition of the cylinder bores. If these are scratched, ovalised or excessively worn a rebore will be necessary. If the reboring operation would remove too much metal, dry cylinder liners can be fitted. In either case, the work must be carried out by a specialist service station.

1:5 Timing belt renewal

Refer to **Section 1:7** and remove the camshaft cover. Remove the sparking plugs so that the engine can be turned easily, then align the engine so that No 4 (flywheel end) cylinder is at TDC on the firing stroke. To do this, either push the car forward in top gear or rotate the engine by means of a spanner on the crankshaft pulley nut, turning in a clockwise direction when viewed from the pulley end. The engine is correctly aligned when the timing mark on the crankshaft pulley aligns with the TDC mark on the cover, with the camshaft pulley timing mark aligned with the cast finger on the support and the cam lobes for No 4 cylinder pointing upwards by equal amounts. The camshaft pulley timing mark is visible through the hole provided in the cover. The engine will be aligned correctly once in every two revolutions. **Never turn the engine backwards as slack will develop in the timing belt and this may cause the belt to jump the pulley teeth and affect engine timing.**

Refer to **FIG 1:17**. Remove the upper bolts securing timing cover 1, then remove the righthand guard from beneath the engine and remove the cover lower securing bolt. Detach the cover.

Loosen alternator fixings 4 and 5, swing the alternator towards the engine and remove drive belt 3. With top gear selected and the handbrake applied to lock the engine, slacken the securing nut for crankshaft pulley 2. Remove the nut and the pulley, collecting the locating key.

On models with emission control systems, remove the two bolts through the rear of air pump 8 and support brackets 7, then loosen the bolt through the top of the pump. Move the pump to slacken its toothed drive belt, then remove the belt from the pulleys.

Check that the timing marks are correctly aligned as previously described, rotating the engine forwards again to realign, if necessary. Refer to **Chapter 3** and remove the distributor, without turning the engine at all. Refer to **FIG 1:18** and loosen the idler pulley locknut 1. Push-in on the support to release belt tension, then tighten the locknut to secure tensioner in retracted position. Remove the toothed timing belt 3, first from the idler pulley then from the remaining pulleys. **Do not turn either the camshaft or crankshaft while the belt is removed, otherwise valves may contact pistons and cause serious damage.**

Install the new belt first over the crankshaft pulley, then over the auxiliary shaft and camshaft pulleys, keeping the belt taut between pulleys. Note that the camshaft pulley may have to be turned very slightly to engage pulley and belt teeth correctly. Carefully twist the belt over the idler pulley, taking care to avoid kinking or straining the belt, which may damage the internal construction. Make sure that the timing marks are still correctly aligned, removing the belt and adjusting slightly if necessary. Installation of the timing belt is shown in **FIG 1:19**.

Slacken idler pulley locknut 4 and allow tensioner to take up slack in the belt, then retighten the nut. Push the car forwards in gear so that the engine is rotated through half a turn of the crankshaft, then carry out the tensioner setting again as just described. Now push the car forward to turn the engine through another half turn until the TDC point for No 4 cylinder is reached, then check for exact alignment of all timing marks. If incorrect, the timing belt must be removed again and the tensioning procedure restarted. If correct, finally reset the tensioner as before, then tighten idler pulley locknut to 4.5kgm (32.5lb ft).

Refit the remaining components in the reverse order of removal, tensioning air pump drive belt as described in **Section 1:14** (where fitted) and alternator drive belt as described in **Chapter 4**. On completion, refit the distributor and adjust ignition timing as described in **Chapter 3**.

1:6 Valve timing

Valve timing can be checked by rotating the engine until it is set at the firing point for No 4 cylinder with the mark on the crankshaft pulley correctly aligned with the TDC mark, as described in **Section 1:5**. The mark on the camshaft pulley should then be correctly aligned with the finger on the support (see **FIG 1:19**). If alignment is incorrect by a small amount, remove the timing belt as described in **Section 1:5**, turn the camshaft pulley slightly until correctly aligned, then refit the belt. Note that camshaft

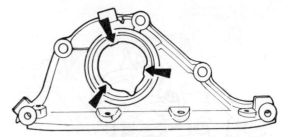

FIG 1:16   Aligning crankcase cover, timing gear side

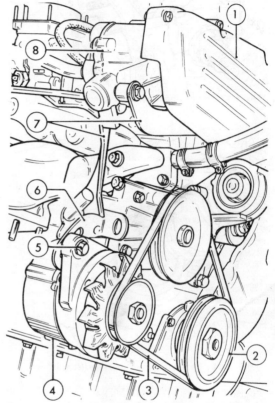

FIG 1:17   Timing cover removal

FIG 1:18   Timing belt removal

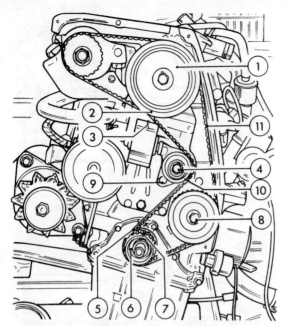

FIG 1:19   Timing belt, pulleys and timing marks

Key to Fig 1:19   1 Camshaft pulley   2 Timing mark   3 Fixed timing mark   4 Tensioner nut   5 Fixed timing mark   6 Crankshaft pulley   7 Timing mark   8 Auxiliary shaft pulley   9 Tensioner pivot   10 Idler pulley   11 Toothed belt

and crankshaft pulleys must not be turned independently by more than a few degrees unless the camshaft is removed from the cylinder head or the cylinder head and camshaft assembly is removed from the block, otherwise valves may contact pistons and cause serious damage.

If valve timing is to be set after engine overhaul procedures have been carried out, make sure that the crankshaft timing marks are correctly aligned, with the piston for No 4 cylinder (flywheel end) at the top of its bore, before installing the cylinder head or camshaft,

whichever is the case. Note that the camshaft pulley must be fitted to the camshaft and rotated to the correct position, so that the timing marks will align as shown in **FIG 1:19**, before cylinder head and/or camshaft assembly is fitted and tightened down. If this is not done, engine damage may occur. Final installation of the timing belt is described in **Section 1:5**. Note that the ignition timing must always be checked and reset as necessary after carrying out valve timing procedures (see **Chapter 3**).

1:7 Camshaft removal and refitting

Removal:

Refer to **Section 1:8** and carry out the necessary removal instructions to disconnect all items from the camshaft cover and housing, noting that there is no need to drain the cooling system. Remove the fixing nuts and washers and detach the camshaft cover and gasket. Remove the timing belt as described in **Section 1:5**.

Slacken the nuts securing camshaft housing to cylinder head alternately and evenly to avoid distortion, then remove the nuts and washers and lift off the camshaft housing assembly and gasket.

Lock the camshaft pulley against rotation by suitable means, then straighten the tab washer and slacken the pulley securing bolt. Remove bolt, washer and pulley. Remove the cover and gasket from the opposite end of the housing, noting the locations of drive gear components on early models with distributor driven from camshaft. Carefully withdraw the camshaft from housing, towards the side opposite the pulley, taking care not to damage bearings or cam lobes.

Examine the cams and bearing surfaces for wear or damage. The camshaft should be renewed if excessive wear or scoring is evident, or if the shaft is out of true. **FIG 1:20** shows the dimensions in millimetres for the camshaft bearings and journals. Note that, due to the need for special equipment, the renewal of camshaft bearings should be carried out by a service station. The camshaft housing oil seal should be renewed if worn, damaged or leaking by carefully removing the old seal from the bore and driving a new seal squarely into place.

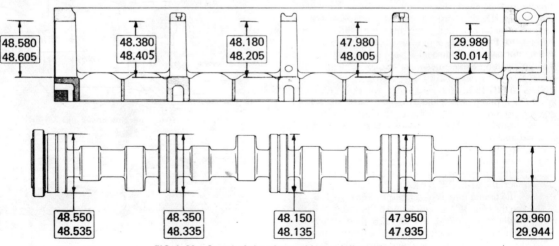

FIG 1:20   Camshaft bearing and journal dimensions

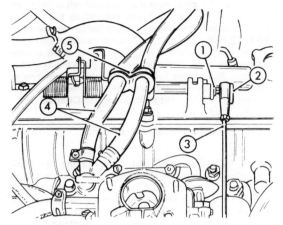

FIG 1:21 Disconnecting hoses and throttle linkage

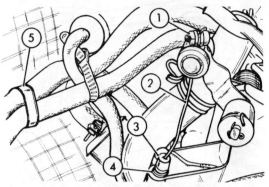

FIG 1:22 Disconnecting accelerator cable

Refitting:

Lubricate the cam lobes, journals and oil seal lips with engine oil, then carefully insert the camshaft taking care not to damage the oil seal. Align the pulley with the dowel on the camshaft, fit a new tab washer, tighten the bolt and lock by bending up the tab. Refit the camshaft housing in the reverse order of removal, making sure that the pulley is correctly aligned (see **Section 1:6**) before fitting and tightening down. Use new gaskets throughout and tighten fixings alternately and evenly to avoid distortion. Before installing the camshaft cover, check and if necessary adjust valve clearances as described in **Section 1:10**.

1:8 Removing and refitting cylinder head

Removal:

Refer to **Chapter 4** and drain the cooling system, then remove the air cleaner assembly as described in **Chapter 2**. Refer to **FIG 1:21** and disconnect the two fuel hoses 4 from carburetter, then pull hoses and grommets out of bracket 5. Slide spring clip 2 from ball connector 1 for throttle rod 3, then disconnect rod from connector. Disconnect HT leads from sparking plugs. Disconnect vacuum hose for distributor from fitting at cylinder head.

Refer to **FIG 1:22** and remove stop bolt 1 from accelerator cable 2. Slide seal 3 from cable, then remove the clip securing cable to camshaft cover 4. Remove the cable.

Refer to **FIG 1:23** and disconnect water outlet hose 1, inlet hose 2, pump hose 3 and expansion tank hose 4 from union 5. Remove bolt securing reaction rod 6 in bracket and move rod away from work area. Disconnect hose 7 from exhaust shroud.

Refer to **FIG 1:24** and disconnect wires from thermo-switch 4 on carburetter. Disconnect hose 5 and, if an air pump is fitted, disconnect hoses 1 and 3 from air pump 2. Disconnect the exhaust pipe at the manifold flange. Remove the timing belt as described in **Section 1:5**.

Slacken the cylinder head retaining bolts and nuts in the reverse order of that shown in **FIG 1:25**, then remove the bolts and nuts and lift off the cylinder head complete with exhaust manifold, inlet manifold and carburetter. Remove and discard the cylinder head gasket.

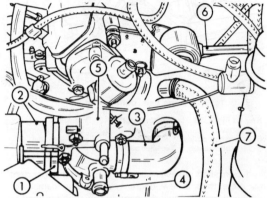

FIG 1:23 Disconnecting hoses and reaction rod

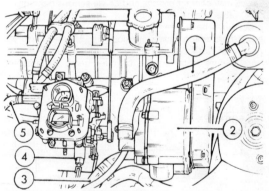

FIG 1:24 Disconnecting hoses and wiring

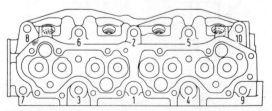

FIG 1:25 Cylinder head bolt and nut tightening sequence

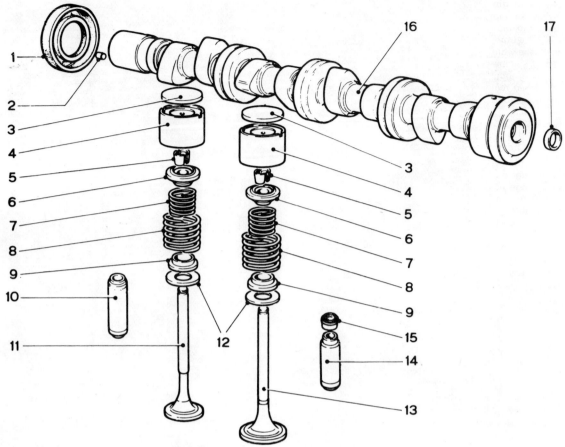

FIG 1:26 Camshaft and valve gear components

Key to Fig 1:26   1 Seal   2 Pin   3 Adjusting capsule   4 Tappet   5 Cotters   6 Valve spring seat   7 Inner valve spring
8 Outer valve spring   9 Valve spring seat   10 Valve guide   11 Exhaust valve   12 Washers   13 Inlet valve   14 Valve guide
15 Seal   16 Camshaft   17 Bush

Refitting:

Clean all traces of old gasket material from the head and block, taking care not to damage the joint face of the light alloy cylinder head. Fit a new gasket to the cylinder block, making sure that the gasket is the right way up by checking that each hole in the gasket matches the appropriate bore in the cylinder block surface. Make sure that the engine is correctly aligned as described in **Section 1:5** and the camshaft sprocket correctly aligned as described in **Section 1:6** before installing the cylinder head. Fit the head in place, maintaining camshaft sprocket alignment, then install the retaining bolts and nuts finger tight. Tighten the bolts and nuts in two stages, first to a torque of 29lb ft then to 61.5lb ft, keeping to the order shown in **FIG 1:25**. Refit the remaining components in the reverse order of removal, making sure that neither camshaft nor crankshaft are turned before the timing belt has been correctly installed as described in **Section 1:5**. On completion, check ignition timing as described in **Chapter 3** then fill and bleed the cooling system as described in **Chapter 4**.

1:9 Servicing cylinder head and valves

Dismantling:

Remove the thermostat housing complete with thermostat and remove the toothed belt protective cover. Refer to **Section 1:7** and remove the camshaft and housing assembly.

FIG 1:26 shows camshaft and valve gear components. **Note that all valve gear components must be marked or stored in the correct order for refitting**

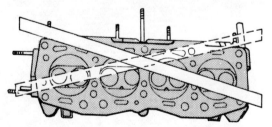

FIG 1:27   Checking cylinder head for distortion

in their original positions if not to be renewed.
Remove the tappets with their adjusting capsules, then remove exhaust manifold and inlet manifold with carburetter from cylinder head. Discard the flange gaskets and use new ones when reassembling.

Use a suitable valve spring compressor to remove the valve gear from the cylinder head. With the springs compressed, remove the split taper collets then remove the compressor tool and collect the valve, springs, spring seats and washers.

Servicing:

Cylinder head:

Check the cylinder head for distortion, using a metal straightedge on the joint face as shown in **FIG 1:27**. With straightedge held against the surface, it should not be possible to fit a 0.002in (0.05mm) feeler gauge between the straightedge and joint face at any point. If distortion is evident, the cylinder head should be resurfaced at a specialist service station. Note that the amount of metal that can be removed in this operation is limited. After resurfacing, depth of combustion chambers should be checked using special gauge A.96216. With the shaped gauge held vertically and fitted in the combustion chamber contours, it should not be possible to fit a 0.01in (0.25mm) feeler gauge between either outer shoulder of the gauge and the cylinder head joint face. If depth of any chamber is insufficient, a new cylinder head will be required.

Cylinder head decarbonising and reseating of valves is described later.

Valves:

When the valves have been cleaned of carbon deposits they must be inspected for serviceability. Valves with bent stems or badly burned heads must be renewed. Valves that are pitted can be recut at a service station, but if they are too far gone for this remedial treatment, new valves will be required. The correct valve seat angles are shown in **FIG 1:28**.

Valve guides:

Valve guides that are worn or scored must be renewed. As the guides must be pressed into or out of place, reamed

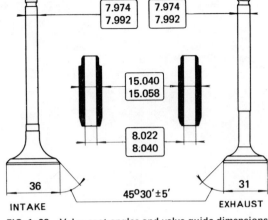

FIG 1:28 Valve seat angles and valve guide dimensions

to obtain the correct running clearance if necessary, then the valve seat recut to ensure concentricity, this work should be carried out by a service station having the necessary special equipment.

Valve seat inserts:

Valve seat inserts that are pitted or burned must be refaced or, if they are too far gone for remedial treatment, renewed. As either operation requires the use of special equipment, this work should be carried out by a service station. The correct valve seat angles at cylinder head inserts are shown in **FIG 1:29**.

Valve springs:

Test the valve springs by referring to **Technical Data** and loading each spring by the stated amount and checking that the compressed length is not less than the figure given. Alternatively, compare the efficiency of the old springs against that of a new spring. To do this, insert both the old and new springs end to end with a metal plate between them into the jaws of a vice. If the old spring has weakened, it will close up first as pressure is applied.

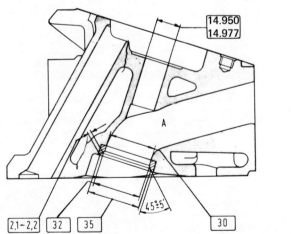
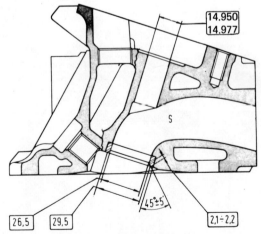

FIG 1:29 Valve seat insert angles for inlet valve (left) and exhaust valve (right)

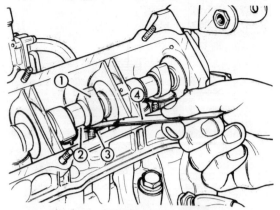

FIG 1:30   Checking valve clearances

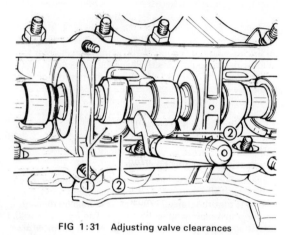

FIG 1:31   Adjusting valve clearances

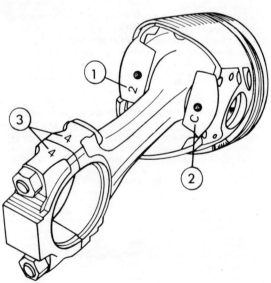

FIG 1:32   Piston and connecting rod assembly

Make sure that the assembly is kept square to prevent the springs from flying from the vice as pressure is applied. Any spring which is distorted, or which is shorter or weaker than standard, should be renewed. However, it is recommended that if any spring is defective all valve springs are renewed as a complete set.

Decarbonising and valve reseating:

Avoid the use of sharp tools which could damage the light alloy cylinder head and piston surfaces. Remove all traces of carbon deposits from the combustion chambers, inlet and exhaust ports and joint faces. If the pistons have not been removed and cleaned during previous engine dismantling, plug the waterways and oil holes in the top surface for the cylinder block with pieces of rag to prevent the entry of dirt, then clean the carbon from piston crowns. If the engine is turned to facilitate cleaning of pistons, make sure that it is correctly realigned as described in **Section 1:5** before the cylinder head is refitted.

The manufacturers do not recommend grinding the valves to their seats using carborundum paste in the conventional manner. Instead, valves and seats should be recut to the correct angles at a service station having the necessary special equipment. A special gauge is also necessary to check that the valve stem height above the cylinder head is correct when the work is complete.

Reassembly:

This is a reversal of the removal procedure. Lubricate the moving parts with engine oil during reassembly, paying particular attention to the camshaft lobes and bearings and the valve stems. Make sure that all valve gear components are refitted in their original positions unless renewed. On completion, check valve clearances and adjust if necessary, as described in the next section.

1:10 Valve clearance adjustment

The correct adjustment of valve clearances is important as it affects engine timing and performance considerably. Excessive clearance will reduce valve lift and opening duration and reduce engine performance, causing excessive wear on the valve gear components and noisy operation. Insufficient or zero clearance will again affect engine timing and, in some circumstances, can hold the valve clear of its seat. This will result in much reduced performance and the possibility of burned valves and seats. Valve clearances should be checked at the intervals recommended in the manufacturer's service schedule as routine maintenance and, additionally, whenever the cylinder head has been serviced. Checking should also be carried out at any time when valve gear noise is noticed.

The valve clearances must be checked and adjusted when the engine is cold, so allow it to cool down completely before proceeding. The correct clearances are 0.012in (0.30mm) for inlet valves and 0.016in (0.40mm) for exhaust valves.

Remove the air cleaner and the camshaft cover. Turn the engine in the forward direction by pushing the car forwards in top gear or by means of a spanner on the crankshaft pulley nut, until the cam lobe above the first valve to be checked is vertical, as shown at 1 in **FIG 1:30**. In either case, the engine will be easier to turn if the sparking plugs are removed first. Check the clearance

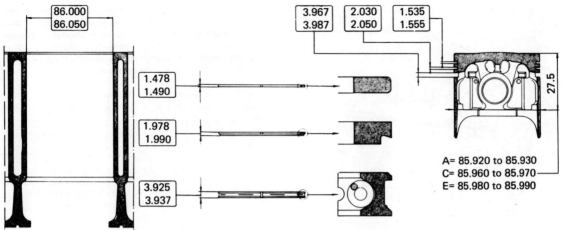

FIG 1 :33   Piston ring and groove widths

between cam 1 and adjusting capsule 2 in tappet 3, using a feeler gauge 4 of the correct thickness. Work in this manner until all valve clearances have been checked, noting the clearance reading for each valve as it is taken. If any clearance is incorrect, adjustment must be carried out in the following manner.

Turn the engine until the cam lobe above the valve in question is pointing downwards, holding the valve fully open. Position special tool A.60421 or similar to lock the tappet in the fully depressed position, then turn the engine until the cam lobe is vertical as shown in **FIG 1 :31**. Use compressed air to eject the adjusting capsule from the tappet, applying the air jet through the tappet slot. Alternatively, use a suitable pointed tool to remove the capsule.

Note the number on the removed capsule and determine the thickness required for the new capsule, using the clearance measurement taken earlier. Select a new capsule of the correct thickness and fit it to the tappet. Turn the engine until the cam lobe contacts the capsule, then remove the holding tool and recheck the clearance. Adjusting capsules are available in thicknesses from 3.25 to 4.70mm, in steps of 0.05mm.

1 :11   Pistons and connecting rods

Pistons and connecting rods can be removed with the engine in situ, but if it is later found that attention to the cylinder bores or crankshaft journals is required, it will be necessary to remove the engine as described in **Section 1 :2**.

Removal :

Remove the cylinder head as described in **Section 1 :8** and the sump as described in **Section 1 :12**. Turn the engine by means of a spanner on the crankshaft pulley securing nut to bring each big-end bearing in turn to an accessible position. Check for a ridge of carbon at the top of the cylinder bore, carefully scraping this away if necessary, taking care not to damage the bore surface. Remove the connecting rod cap nuts and detach the cap with lower shell bearing. Release the connecting rod from the crankpin and carefully push piston and connecting rod

assembly through the top of the bore to remove. Keep all parts, including the bearing shells, in the correct order for refitting in their original positions and the same way round, if not to be renewed. **FIG 1 :32** shows piston gudgeon pin bore class mark 1, piston class letter 2 and mating numbers for connecting rod and cap 3. When the assemblies are installed, the matching numbers 3 must face towards the auxiliary shaft side of the engine.

Servicing :

Connecting rods and bearings :

Examine connecting rods carefully and renew any found damaged or distorted. If there has been a big-end bearing failure, the crankpin must be examined for damage and for transfer of metal to its surface. The oilway in the crankshaft must be checked to ensure that there is no obstruction. Big-end bearing clearance can be checked by the use of Plastigage, which is the trade name for a precisely calibrated plastic filament. The filament is laid along the bearing to be measured for working clearance, the bearing cap fitted and the nuts tightened to the correct torque. The bearing is then dismantled and the width of the flattened filament measured with the scale supplied with the material. The bearing clearance can then be read off the scale. Both main and big-end bearing clearances are measured in the same manner.

Note that each main bearing must be measured separately and that none of the remaining caps must be fitted during the operation. The bearing surfaces must be clean and free from oil and the crankshaft must not be turned during the measuring procedure. The point at which the measurement is taken must be close to the respective dead centre position and no hammer blows must be applied to the bearing or cap.

Place a length of plastic filament identical to the width of the bearing along the crankshaft journal, then fit the main or big-end bearing cap with bearing shells and tighten to the specified torque.

Remove the bearing cap and measure the width of the flattened filament to obtain the running clearance for that bearing. Clearances are given in **Technical Data**. If running clearance is too high, new bearing shells must be

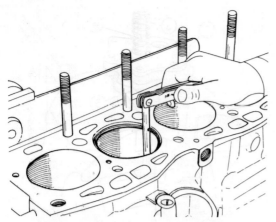

FIG 1:34   Checking piston ring fitted gap

selected by the measurement procedure to bring running clearance to within specified limits.

If crankshaft bearing journals are excessively worn or damaged in any way, the journals must be reground to accept suitable undersize bearing shells, this being a specialist job.

Pistons and rings:

Clean carbon deposits from the piston crowns, taking care not to damage the light alloy surfaces, then gently ease the rings from their grooves and remove them over the tops of the pistons. Keep all rings in the correct order for refitting in their original positions, if not to be renewed. Clean carbon from the piston ring grooves, for which job a piece broken from an old piston ring and ground to a chisel point will prove an ideal tool. Inspect the pistons for score marks or any signs of seizure, which would dictate renewal. **FIG 1:33** shows correct widths for piston rings and ring grooves.

Fit the piston rings one at a time to the bore from which they were removed, pushing them down with the correct inverted piston to ensure squareness. Measure the gap between the ends of the ring while it is positioned in the bore, using feeler gauges as shown in **FIG 1:34**. Remove the ring from the bore and refer to **FIG 1:35**. Fit the ring 1

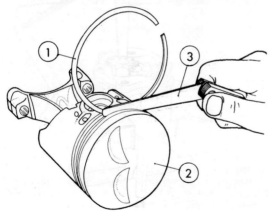

FIG 1:35   Checking piston ring side clearance

into groove of piston 2 from which it was removed, then measure side clearance using feeler gauges 3. Compare the measurements taken with the figures given in **Technical Data**. If the clearance measurement in either test is at or near the wear limit, new rings must be fitted. Excessive ring clearance can be responsible for high oil consumption and poor engine performance.

Check the cylinder bores for score marks and remove glaze and carbon deposits. Badly scored or worn surfaces will dictate a rebore to accept new pistons, this being a specialist job. The fitting of new pistons to connecting rods must be carried out by a fully equipped service station, due to the need for special tools and press equipment to remove and refit the gudgeon pins. Check the clearance of each piston in its bore. To do this, measure the outside diameter of the piston and the inside diameter of the bore and compare the two figures. Piston diameter should always be measured at right angles to the gudgeon pin bore. If clearances are excessive, new pistons may be all that is required if the bores are in good condition, but if the bores are worn reboring at a specialist service station will be necessary.

Refitting:

This is a reversal of the removal procedure. Carefully fit the rings to the correct piston grooves and stagger the ring end gaps equally around the piston circumference. Make sure that the assemblies are the correct way round, with connecting rod and cap markings facing towards auxiliary shaft. Lubricate the pistons with engine oil and use a suitable piston ring clamp when entering the rings into the cylinder bores. Push each piston down the bore until the connecting rod with shell bearing can be fitted over the crankpin, then lubricate the shell bearings and install the cap with lower bearing, making sure that it is the correct way round. Fit the cap nuts and tighten to the specified torque.

1:12 Lubrication system

Sump removal:

This work can be carried out with the engine in situ. Raise the rear of the car for access to the underside and support safely on floor stands. Fit a suitable engine support tool or attach suitable engine lifting equipment and tighten sufficiently to take the weight of engine and transmission assembly. Remove the lower crossmember which supports the engine. Remove the drain plug and allow the sump oil to drain into a suitable container, then refit and tighten the plug.

Remove the bolts and washers securing sump to crankcase, then detach the sump and remove and discard the gasket. If necessary, remove the inner plate from sump.

Refitting:

Clean sludge from inside the sump and clean all traces of old gasket material from sump and crankcase joint faces. Install the sump, using a new gasket, tightening the fixing bolts alternately and evenly to avoid distortion. Refit the crossmember and remove the engine lifting equipment, then refill the sump with oil to the correct level on the dipstick. Run the engine and check for leaks at the sump gasket, then switch off and allow the oil to drain down into the sump before rechecking the level.

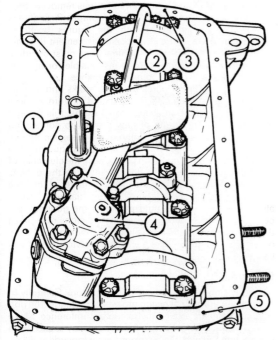

FIG 1:36 Oil pump removal

Key to Fig 1:36 1, 2 Oil return pipes 3 Flywheel end cover plate 4 Oil pump 5 Timing gear end cover plate

Oil pump:

Removal:

Remove the sump as described previously. Refer to **FIG 1:36**. Remove the three fixing bolts and detach oil pump 4 complete with strainer assembly.

Servicing:

Remove the fixing screws and detach strainer assembly from oil pump. Thoroughly clean oil and dirt from the assembly, blowing through the pipe and strainer with compressed air. Make sure that all dirt is removed from beneath relief valve 4 and pump housing 5 (see **FIG 1:37**). Check the relief valve spring for damage or distortion. Free length of the spring should be 40.2mm and length should not be less than 21mm under a load of 5.0kg. Renew the spring if any faults are found.

Check pump internal clearances using feeler gauges and a metal straightedge. Backlash between the two gears should be 0.006in (0.15mm), with a wear limit of 0.01in (0.25mm). Check clearance between gears and housing joint face as shown in **FIG 1:38**. Clearance between gear surface and straightedge should be 0.008 to 0.040in (0.020 to 0.105mm), with a wear limit of 0.06in (0.15mm). Check gear tooth to housing clearance as shown in **FIG 1:39**. This should be 0.004 to 0.007in (0.11 to 0.18mm), with a wear limit of 0.01in (0.25mm). Excessive clearance in any test will dictate renewal of the pump gears, pump housing or both. Renew the pump cover if the inner surface is worn or scored. When the gears are refitted to the housing, make sure that they rotate freely.

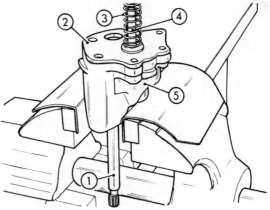

FIG 1:37 Oil pump with strainer removed

Key to Fig 1:37 1 Pump drive shaft 2 Cover 3 Relief valve spring 4 Relief valve 5 Housing

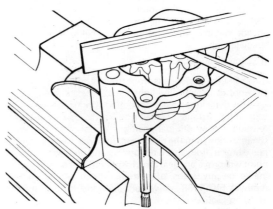

FIG 1:38 Checking pump gear to cover clearance

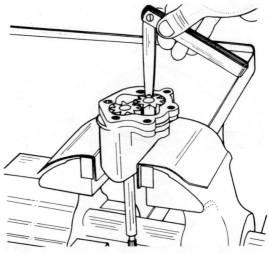

FIG 1:39 Checking pump gear to housing clearance

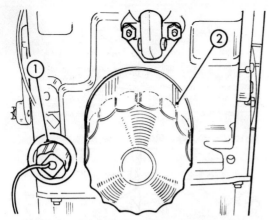

FIG 1:40   Oil pressure sender unit 1 and oil filter 2

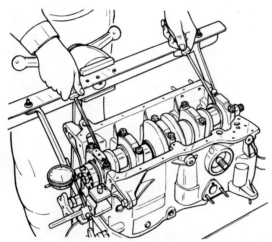

FIG 1:41   Checking crankshaft end play

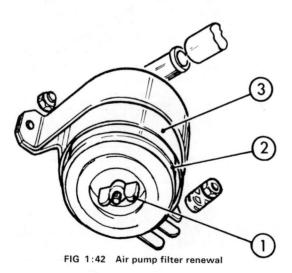

FIG 1:42   Air pump filter renewal

Refitting:

This is a reversal of the removal procedure, lubricating the pump gears with engine oil and using new gaskets throughout.

Oil filter renewal:

The oil filter is of the renewable element fullflow type, a bypass valve being incorporated in the filter mounting to allow oil to pass directly from the pump to the engine, bypassing the filter, if the filter element should become blocked. The filter should be renewed at the intervals recommended in the manufacturer's service schedule.

Oil filter installation is shown in **FIG 1:40**. Before removal, place an oil tray beneath the unit as some oil will escape even if the sump has been drained. Unscrew the filter, using a strap type tool if it proves difficult to turn by hand. Discard the used cartridge.

Clean the mounting on the engine then lightly coat the seal on the new filter cartridge with engine oil. Make sure that the seal is correctly fitted, then screw the new filter into place until it just contacts the seating. From this point, tighten a further three-quarters of a turn by hand only. Do not overtighten the filter or oil leaks may result. On completion, start the engine and check for oil leaks around the filter unit. Switch off the engine, then check and top up the oil level to compensate for that used to fill the new filter element.

1:13 Crankshaft, bearings and flywheel

Crankshaft removal:

Remove the engine as described in **Section 1:2** then dismantle as described in **Section 1:3**. Before removing the crankshaft, check end play as shown in **FIG 1:41**, using a suitable dial gauge assembly. Use two screwdrivers to lever the crankshaft from one end of its travel to the other and note the total gauge reading. Alternatively, lever the crankshaft as far towards the timing gear end as possible, then use feeler gauges to check clearance between crankshaft flange and thrust washer at flywheel end. End play should be 0.0021 to 0.0104in (0.055 to 0.265mm). Excessive end float will dictate the fitting of new thrust washers when the crankshaft is refitted. Remove the fixing bolts and the main bearing caps, keeping the caps and lower shell bearings in the correct order for refitting in their original positions, if not to be renewed. Lift out the crankshaft, then collect the upper shell bearings and keep in the correct order. Crankshaft bearing clearance can be checked by the use of Plastigage, as described in **Section 1:11**.

Refitting:

This is a reversal of the removal procedure, making sure that the retaining tongues of the shell bearings are free in the housings and that the shells protrude by the same amount on each side of the bearings. Fit the top half thrust washer in place, ensuring that the anti-friction face, which has oil slots, is against the crankshaft shoulder. Lubricate shell bearings and thrust washers with engine oil. Refit the remaining components in the reverse order of removal.

Flywheel:

The flywheel can be removed with the engine in situ, after the clutch assembly has been removed as described in

Chapter 5. Mark the relationship of flywheel to crankshaft flange before removal, so that it can be refitted in its original position to retain the balance of the assembly. Lock the flywheel against rotation by suitable means, then slacken the retaining bolts. Remove the bolts and lift off the flywheel.

Examine the surface of the flywheel against which the clutch plate operates for cracks or scoring. Slight damage of this nature is unimportant, but deeper damage will dictate resurfacing or renewal. If the ring gear is damaged it can be renewed, but this work should be carried out by a service station having the necessary heating and press equipment.

Refit the flywheel in the reverse order of removal, tightening the retaining bolts alternately and evenly to the specified torque.

1:14 Emission control systems

All models are equipped with crankcase emission control systems which operate to ensure that harmful vapours from the crankcase are not vented to atmosphere. The valves in the system allow fresh air to enter the crankcase for ventilation purposes, but the gases are purged through a pipe leading to the air cleaner assembly. Gases are then drawn through the engine inlet manifold to be burnt with the incoming charge in the combustion chambers. The system requires very little maintenance, apart from a regular check on condition of hoses and valves and periodic cleaning of these components.

USA export models are additionally fitted with an exhaust emission control system to ensure that the CO (carbon monoxide) content of the exhaust gas is maintained at the low level required by legislation. The system incorporates an air pump, driven by toothed belt from the camshaft pulley, which pumps a metered quantity of air through a series of pipes and valves into the engine exhaust manifold. This additional air ensures that exhaust gases are burnt completely, preventing harmful emissions which can result from incomplete combustion. The items of maintenance and adjustment given in this section should be carried out at the intervals recommended in the manufacturer's service schedule, but major faults in system operation should be referred to a fully equipped service station having the necessary diagnostic test facilities.

Air pump filter renewal:

Refer to **FIG 1:42**. Remove wing nut 1 at bottom of filter housing 3, then remove and discard filter element 2. Install a new element, refit the housing and tighten the wing nut.

Air pump drive belt tensioning:

Tension of the air pump drive belt should be similar to that of the camshaft drive belt, the latter being automatically set by the tensioner assembly (see **Section 1:5**). If the air pump drive belt tension is found to be incorrect when compared with the camshaft drive belt, slacken the air pump mounting bolts, move the pump away from the engine as necessary, then tighten the bolts and recheck.

Air pump removal:

Refer to **FIG 1:43**. Disconnect hoses 1 and 4 from air pump, then remove timing belt cover 2 as described in

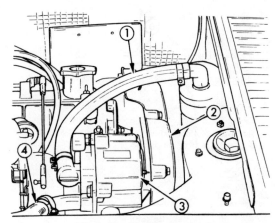

FIG 1:43 Air pump removal

Section 1:5. Remove the bolts from support brackets to rear of air pump 3, then remove bolt securing pump to bracket. Disconnect the drive belt and remove the pump. Refitting is a reversal of the removal procedure, tensioning the belt as described previously.

1:15 Fault diagnosis

(a) Engine will not start

1 Defective coil
2 Faulty distributor capacitor
3 Dirty, pitted or incorrectly set contact points
4 Ignition leads loose or insulation faulty
5 Water on plug leads
6 Battery discharged or terminals corroded
7 Faulty or jammed starter
8 Sparking plug leads wrongly connected
9 Vapour lock in fuel pipes
10 Defective fuel pump
11 Over choking or 'pumping' accelerator pedal
12 Under choking
13 Blocked fuel filter or carburetter jets
14 Leaking valves
15 Sticking valves
16 Valve timing incorrect
17 Ignition timing incorrect

(b) Engine stops

1 Check 1, 2, 3, 4, 10, 11, 12, 13, 14, 15 in (a)
2 Retarded ignition
3 Weak mixture
4 Water in fuel system
5 Fuel tank vent blocked
6 Incorrect valve clearances

(c) Engine idles badly

1 Check 2 and 6 in (b)
2 Air leak at manifold joints
3 Slow running jet blocked or out of adjustment
4 Air leak in carburetter
5 Over rich mixture
6 Worn piston rings
7 Worn valve stems or stem bores
8 Weak valve springs

(d) Engine misfires

1 Check 1, 2, 3, 4, 5, 8, 10, 13, 14, 15, 16, 17 in (a) ; 2, 3, 4, 6 in (b)
2 Weak or broken valve springs

(e) Engine overheats (see Chapter 4)

(f) Compression low

1 Check 14, 15 in (a) ; 7, 8 in (c) ; 2 in (d)
2 Worn piston ring grooves
3 Scored or worn cylinder bores

(g) Engine lacks power

1 Check 3, 10, 11, 13, 14, 15, 16, 17 in (a) ; 2, 3, 4, 6 in (b) ; 7, 8 in (c) ; 2 in (d) ; also check (e) and (f)
2 Leaking joint washers or gaskets
3 Fouled sparking plugs
4 Automatic advance not working

(h) Burnt valves or seats

1 Check 14, 15 in (a) ; 6 in (b) ; 2 in (d) ; also check (e)
2 Excessive carbon around valve seat and head

(j) Sticking valves

1 Check 2 in (d)
2 Bent valve stems
3 Scored valve stems
4 Incorrect valve clearance

(k) Excessive cylinder wear

1 Check 11 in (a)
2 Lack of oil
3 Dirty oil
4 Piston rings gummed or broken
5 Badly fitting piston rings
6 Connecting rod bent

(l) Excessive oil consumption

1 Check 6, 7 in (c) and check (k)
2 Ring gaps too wide
3 Oil return holes in piston blocked
4 Scored cylinders
5 Oil level too high
6 External oil leaks

(m) Crankshaft and connecting rod bearing failure

1 Check 2 in (k)
2 Restricted oilways
3 Worn journals or crankpins
4 Loose bearing caps
5 Extremely low oil pressure
6 Damaged or faulty connecting rod

(n) Engine vibration

1 Loose alternator bolts
2 Fan blades out of balance
3 Faulty or loose engine mountings
4 Exhaust pipe mountings too tight

CHAPTER 2

THE FUEL SYSTEM

2:1 Description
2:2 Routine maintenance
2:3 Air cleaner
2:4 Carburetter cooling fan
2:5 Fuel filter
2:6 Fuel pump

2:7 Carburetter tuning and adjustment
2:8 Carburetter removal and refitting
2:9 Carburetter overhaul
2:10 Emission control system
2:11 Fault diagnosis

2:1 Description

Weber carburetters are fitted to all models covered by this manual, but carburetter type, specifications and type of choke unit (manual or automatic) vary according to year of vehicle manufacture and market territory. In all cases, a mechanical fuel pump, operated by a short pushrod from an eccentric on the engine auxiliary shaft, supplies fuel from the tank to the carburetter through a series of pipes and flexible hoses.

Paper cartridge type air filter elements are used, contained in a casing attached to the carburetter intake. Fuel is filtered through a renewable cartridge type line filter and, additionally, through gauze type filters in fuel pump and carburetter units.

USA export models are equipped with a fuel evaporative emission control system as described in **Section 2:10**, to prevent fuel vapour from escaping into the atmosphere, as required by legislation.

2:2 Routine maintenance

At the intervals recommended in the manufacturer's service schedule, the air cleaner element and fuel line filter element should be renewed and the fuel pump filter gauze removed and cleaned. On models so equipped, the fuel evaporative emission control system should be serviced as described in **Section 2:10**.

2:3 Air cleaner

To renew the air filter element, refer to **FIG 2:1** and remove the three nuts 1, then lift off cover 2. Remove and discard air filter element 1 shown in **FIG 2:2**. Wipe the inside of casing and cover to remove oil and dirt, making sure that no foreign matter enters the carburetter air intakes, then reassemble using a new filter element.

To remove the air cleaner assembly complete, remove cover and filter element as described previously then refer to **FIG 2:1**. Loosen clamp securing air hose 3 to non-return valve 7, then disconnect hose and move it clear of air duct. Loosen clamp 5 securing air duct 4 to carburetter cooling fan 6. Remove nut and washer securing bracket 9 to engine camshaft cover, then disconnect bypass hose 8 from air cleaner. Disconnect hose from bottom of air cleaner. Release the tab washers and remove the four nuts shown at 3 in **FIG 2:2**, then remove air cleaner and fresh air duct assembly.

Refit the air cleaner assembly in the reverse order of removal, using new tab washers if the originals are not in

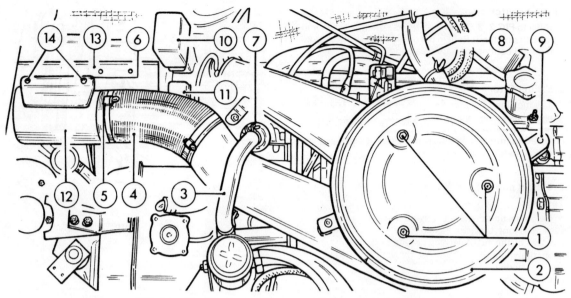

FIG 2:1   Air cleaner and carburetter cooling system installation

Key to Fig 2:1   1 Nuts   2 Air cleaner cover   3 Air hose   4 Air duct   5 Clamp   6 Cooling fan   7 Non-return valve
8 Bypass hose   9 Bracket   10 Voltage regulator   11 Fan relay   12 Fan duct   13 Support   14 Screws

good condition. Tighten the nuts securing air cleaner to carburetter alternately and evenly, then turn up the tab washers to secure.

2:4 Carburetter cooling fan

The carburetter cooling fan operates to prevent the carburetter overheating when temperature in the engine compartment rises above a predetermined point. The fan is controlled by a thermoswitch mounted on the base of the carburetter and a relay mounted on the cooling fan support. If the fan will not operate at all, check that the vehicle interior courtesy light operates when one of the doors is opened. If the light does not operate, check the 8

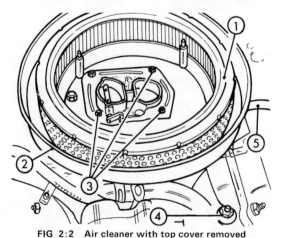

FIG 2:2   Air cleaner with top cover removed

Key to Fig 2:2   1 Filter element   2 Air cleaner   3,4 Nuts
5 Hose

amp fuse in the fusebox and renew if blown (see **Chapter 11**). If the light operates, locate the thermoswitch for the system at the rear of the carburetter. Use a short jumper lead to connect the two thermoswitch wires together. If the fan then runs, the thermostatic switch is faulty and must be renewed. If the fan does not operate, check the wiring and connections in the fan operating circuit. If these are in order the relay must be checked for correct operation, preferably by a service station having special test equipment.

Note that the carburetter cooling fan will continue to run after the engine is switched off and the ignition key removed, provided that carburetter temperature is sufficient to trigger the thermoswitch, this being normal. However, if the fan operates even when the system is cold, disconnect the grey/red wire from the thermostatic switch. If the fan then stops, the switch is faulty and must be renewed. If the fan still runs, reconnect the wire and disconnect the grey/red wire from terminal 85 on relay. If the fan still runs, the relay is defective and must be renewed. If the fan stops, there is a break in the grey/red wire from relay to switch which must be located and repaired.

Cooling fan removal:

Refer to **FIG 2:1**. Disconnect wire from terminal 87 on fan relay 11. Remove the fan relay and voltage regulator 10. Loosen the clamp and disconnect flexible fresh air duct 4 from fan duct. From support 13, remove two nuts at the right front and two bolts from the left rear, then remove fan and support. Remove four screws 14 securing duct to fan, then remove four screws securing fan to support.

Refit the assembly in the reverse order of removal, making sure that the black wire from fan is under mounting nut for fan relay.

Thermoswitch removal:

Refer to **FIG 2:3**. Disconnect wires 2, then unscrew and remove the switch 1. Refit in the reverse order, making sure that wiring connections are clean and tight.

2:5 Fuel filter

The fuel line filter is shown at 1 in **FIG 2:4**. To renew, loosen clips 2 and remove hoses 3. Discard the old filter, then fit a new one in the reverse order of removal. On completion, run the engine and check for leaks at hose connections.

2:6 Fuel pump

Testing:

Before testing the pump, ensure that the fuel tank vent system is not blocked. A blockage is indicated if the removal of the fuel filler cap results in the sound of air being drawn into the tank. If so, the vent system must be checked and cleaned.

If the vent system is clear and it is still suspected that fuel is not reaching the carburetter, disconnect the carburetter feed pipe and hold a suitable container under the end of the pipe. Turn the engine over a few times with the starter and watch for fuel squirting from the end of the pipe, which indicates that the pump is working. If so, check the float needle in the carburetter for possible sticking.

Reduced fuel flow can be caused by blocked fuel pipes or a clogged filter.

If an obstructed pipeline appears to be the cause of the trouble, it may be cleared with compressed air. Disconnect the pipeline at both ends. Do not pass compressed air through the pump or the valves will be damaged. Similarly, make sure that pipes being cleared on cars fitted with emission control system are disconnected at both ends so that compressed air is not passed through system components. If there is an obstruction in the pipe leading from the fuel tank, remove the tank filler cap before blowing the pipe through from the opposite end.

If the pump delivers insufficient fuel, suspect an air leak between the pump and the tank, dirt under the pump valves or faulty valve seatings. Also check for leaks at the pump cover seal and fixing screw washer. If no fuel is delivered, suspect a sticking valve or a faulty pump diaphragm.

Test the action of the pump valves by blowing and sucking at the inlet and outlet points. Do this with the pump in situ, using a suitable piece of pipe connected to the pump inlet and outlet in turn. It should be possible to blow air in through the pump inlet but not to suck air out, and it should be possible to suck air out of the pump outlet but not to blow air in. If the valves do not work properly according to this test, or if the pump is defective in any other way, the pump should be removed and serviced.

Removal:

Refer to **FIG 2:5**. Slacken the clips and detach inlet pipe 1 and outlet pipe 4 from pump unit, plugging the pipes to prevent leakage. Remove two nuts and washers 2 securing pump to engine, then remove pump 3 and collect two gaskets and insulator.

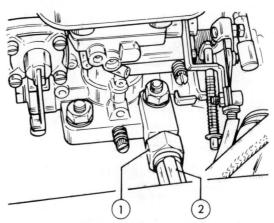

FIG 2:3   Cooling fan thermoswitch removal

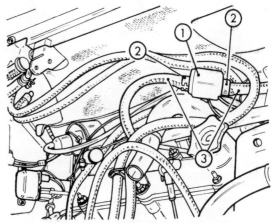

FIG 2:4   Fuel line filter installation

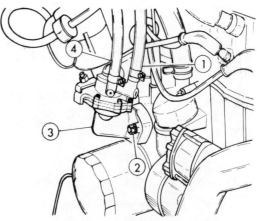

FIG 2:5   Fuel pump removal

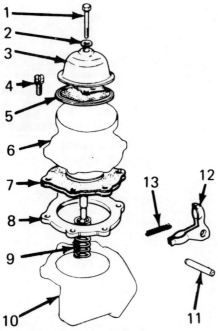

FIG 2:6 Fuel pump components

Key to Fig 2:6 1 Cover screw 2 Washer 3 Cover
4 Screw 5 Filter gauze 6 Upper body 7 Diaphragm
8 Spacer 9 Spring 10 Lower body 11 Pivot pin
12 Control lever 13 Return spring

Servicing:

Note that the fuel filter in the pump can be removed and cleaned without the need for pump removal. To overhaul the pump, dismantle the unit into the order shown in **FIG 2:6**. Thoroughly clean the filter and chamber with clean petrol, using a small brush to remove stubborn deposits. If the filter will not clean up or is damaged in any way it should be renewed.

Check the diaphragm for splits, distortion or hardening of the material. If it is not in perfect condition it should be renewed. Check all other components for wear or damage, renewing parts as necessary. If the valves are defective and do not operate correctly after carefully cleaning with petrol, the valve body must be renewed complete as the valves cannot be renewed separately.

Reassemble the unit in the reverse order of dismantling, lubricating the control lever and pivot with oil. Use new gaskets, lightly coated with grease. Before tightening the screws connecting the upper and lower bodies, operate the control lever through half its travel so that the diaphragm is flat. Hold in this position while alternately and evenly tightening the screws.

Refitting:

This is a reversal of the removal procedure, but adjustments should be carried out in the following manner to ensure correct pump pushrod stroke.

Refer to **FIG 2:7**. Fit a new gasket 3 on the engine then install insulator 4 with a new 0.3mm (0.012in) gasket 2. Fit pushrod 5, then turn the engine until projection **A** of pushrod is at a minimum. This ensures that the pushrod is operating on the back of the cam in the engine. Under these conditions, dimension **A** should be 15.0 to 15.5mm (0.59 to 0.61in). If necessary, install a thicker or thinner gasket 2 to bring pushrod projection to within the limits stated. This done, refit the fuel pump, making sure that the pushrod correctly engages the pump operating lever. Tighten the retaining nuts alternately and evenly to avoid distortion of the flange. Reconnect the fuel pipes, then start the engine and check for fuel leaks at pipe connections.

2:7 Carburetter tuning and adjustment

Adjusting carburetter controls:

Remove the air cleaner assembly for access, as described in **Section 2:3**. Have an assistant operate the accelerator pedal through a full stroke and hold it to the floor. Check that the linkage at the carburetter opens the throttle fully but without strain. Have the accelerator pedal released, then check that the linkage moves freely to the closed position. If adjustment is necessary, slacken the locknut and adjust throttle operating rod as necessary then retighten locknut. Lightly lubricate joints in the linkage.

On models fitted with manual choke unit, operate the control in the car fully then check that the cable has moved the choke linkage at the carburetter to the fully closed position. Return the control to the fully off position, then check that the linkage at the carburetter has returned fully. There should be a small amount of slack in the cable when the control is fully home, to ensure that the choke always releases fully. If adjustment is necessary, slacken the cable clamp at carburetter linkage, adjust cable as necessary,

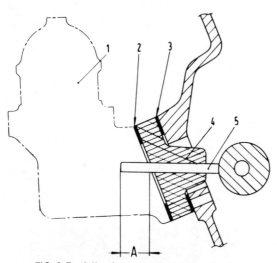

FIG 2:7 Adjusting pump pushrod projection

Key to Fig 2:7 1 Pump 2,3 Gaskets 4 Insulator
5 Pushrod

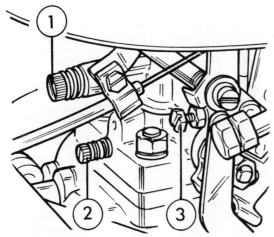

FIG 2:8 Typical carburetter idle adjustment screws, European models

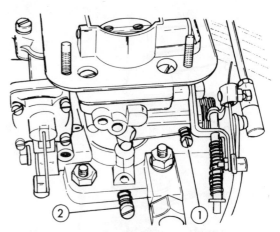

FIG 2:9 Typical carburetter idle adjustment screws, USA export models

then retighten clamp. Lightly lubricate moving parts of linkage.

Slow-running adjustments:

Note that slow-running adjustments will only be effective if the sparking plugs, contact points and ignition system are in good order and the valve clearances are correctly set. On completion, the CO (carbon monoxide) content of the exhaust should be checked and further fine adjustments made to bring the level to within prescribed limits, if necessary. If suitable analytical equipment is not available for this purpose, the CO content should be checked by a service station.

Run the engine until normal operating temperature is reached, this being when the radiator cooling fan starts to operate. This done, switch off the engine then remove the air cleaner assembly as described in **Section 2:3**. Refer to **FIG 2:8** or **2:9**, as appropriate. Note that, on European models, the throttle stop screw 3 is factory-set and must not be adjusted in service.

Start the engine and allow it to idle. The correct idling speed for European models is 850 to 900rev/min, for USA export models it is as marked on the tag provided in the engine compartment. If necessary, adjust screw 1 to obtain the specified idle speed. Now adjust volume control screw 2, a little at a time, to obtain the highest possible idle speed, then readjust idle speed screw 1 to return idle speed to the correct level. Repeat the adjustment procedure until no further gain in speed can be obtained by adjusting screw 2. Final adjustments should now be made at the volume control screw to bring the CO content to within 4.5 per cent by volume for European models, or to the figure stated on the engine compartment tag in the case of USA export models. If this procedure alters the idle speed, readjust at idle speed screw 1 then recheck CO content.

Checking float and needle valve:

Checking of float and needle valve assemblies will be necessary if carburetter flooding is encountered, or if fuel starvation problems are traced to the carburetter. Flooding can be caused by incorrect float level, a damaged or

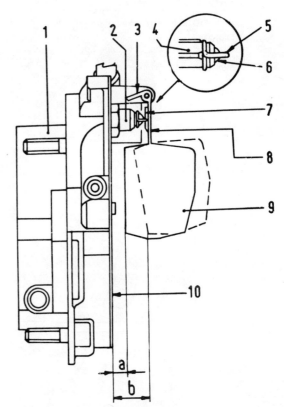

FIG 2:10 Checking float level

Key to Fig 2:10   1 Carburetter cover   2 Needle valve assembly   3 Tang   4 Needle   5 Return hook   6 Moveable ball   7 Tang   8 Float arm   9 Float   10 Gasket

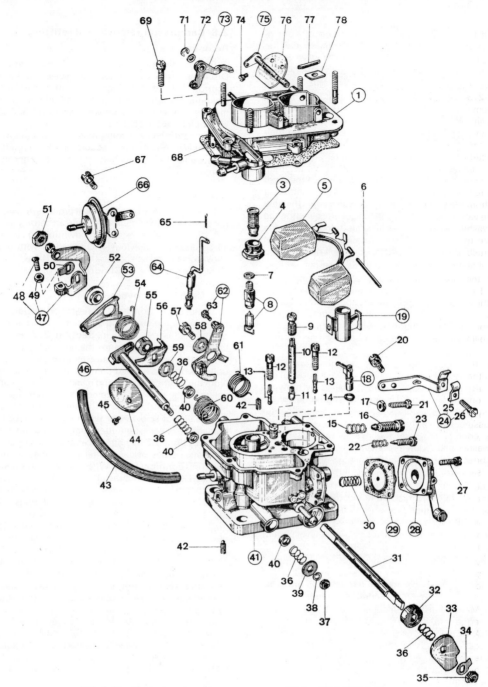

FIG 2:11   Typical carburetter components, Weber 32 DMTRA shown

Key to Fig 2:11   1 Carburetter cover   3 Filter   4 Filter plug   5 Float   6 Float pivot pin   7 Gasket   8 Needle valve
9 Air metering jet   10 Emulsion tube   11 Main jet   12 Idle jet holders   13 Idle jets   14 Gasket   15 Spring   16 Idle
bypass screw   17 Nut   18 Accelerator pump cover   19 Venturi   20, 21 Screws   22 Spring   23 Idle mixture screw
24 to 26 Choke cable support bracket   27 Screw   28 Accelerator pump cover   29 Diaphragm   30 Spring   31 Throttle shaft,
primary   32 Oil vapour distributor   33 Lever   34 Lockwasher   35 Nut   36 Spring   37 Nut   38 Spring washer
39 Washer   40 Bushing   41 Carburetter body   42 Secondary throttle stop screw   43 Hose   44 Throttle plate   45 Screw
46 Throttle shaft, secondary   47 to 49 Throttle lever assembly   50 Lockwasher   51 Nut   52 Bushing   53 Lever   54 Spring
55 Bushing   56 Primary shaft lever   57 Screw   58, 59 Washers   60, 61 Lever   62 Lever   63 Screw   64 Choke rod
65 Cotter pin   66 Choke override   67 Screw   68 Cover gasket   69 Screw   71 Circlip   72 Washer   73 Choke override
control   74 Screw   75 Choke plate shaft   76 Choke plate   77 Clip   78 Dust cover

punctured float, or by a needle valve which is worn or sticking in the open position. Fuel starvation can be caused by incorrect float level or by a needle valve which sticks in the closed position.

Remove the air cleaner assembly as described in **Section 2:3**. Disconnect fuel feed pipe and, on models with automatic choke units, the water pipes from the choke unit. Plug water pipes to prevent leakage. Disconnect carburetter linkages as necessary, noting their positions for correct reassembly, then remove the screws securing carburetter top cover to carburetter body. Lift off the cover, taking care not to damage the floats, then remove and discard the gasket. Carefully remove the pivot pin, then remove the float assembly, carefully unhooking the tang from the wire hook on the needle valve. Unscrew the needle valve housing from the top cover, collecting the sealing washer. Remove the cover plug and extract the filter gauze, then carefully clean the gauze using petrol and a small brush. If the filter is damaged or will not clean up properly, it should be renewed.

Check the floats carefully for signs of damage or leakage. Float leakage can generally be detected by shaking the float and listening for the sound of fuel splash inside, or by immersing the float in warm water and looking for a stream of bubbles which will indicate any point of leakage. Renew the float assembly if any fault is found.

Check the float needle valve assembly carefully, renewing the assembly if there is any sign of a ridge on the tapered valve seat. Check for correct sealing by blowing through from the feed end. The air flow should be cut off completely when the needle is held onto its seat by gentle finger pressure. Renew the assembly if there is any doubt about its condition. Check the needle valve assembly sealing washer and renew if damaged or distorted. Note that the correct sealing washer must always be installed, as this affects control of the fuel level in float chamber.

Refit the fuel filter and sealing plug, then install and tighten the needle valve assembly with sealing washer. Install the float assembly, making sure that the needle valve hook fits correctly over the tang and that the assembly moves freely on the pivot pin. Float level should now be checked in the following manner.

Fit a new gasket to the carburetter top cover, then hold the assembly in a vertical position as shown in **FIG 2:10** so that the float arm rests against the needle valve under its own weight, without depressing the spring-loaded ball in the valve. Measure distance **a** between the gasket surface and upper edge of float. This should be 7.0mm (0.28in) for 32 DATRA carburetter, or 6.0mm (0.24in) for all other units. If necessary, adjust by carefully bending tang 7. Turn the carburetter cover gently to its normal attitude so that the float hangs free. Now check dimension **b**, which should be 15mm (0.59in) in all cases. If necessary, adjust by carefully bending tang 3.

On completion, refit the carburetter top cover in the reverse order of removal, using the new gasket. Tighten the fixing screws alternately and evenly to avoid distortion. Check and if necessary adjust control linkage and make slow running adjustments, as described previously. On models fitted with automatic choke unit, check and if necessary top up and bleed the cooling system as described in **Chapter 4**.

2:8 Carburetter removal and refitting

Removal:

Remove the air cleaner as described in **Section 2:3**. Disconnect the carburetter fuel pipes and the throttle control linkage. On models with manual choke, disconnect the choke cable at carburetter linkage. On models with automatic choke, disconnect and plug the water pipes at the choke unit.

Disconnect wiring from carburetter thermoswitch and disconnect distributor vacuum pipe at carburetter. Remove the fixing nuts and lift the carburetter from inlet manifold, then remove and discard the flange gasket.

Refitting:

This is a reversal of the removal procedure, using a new flange gasket. On completion, carry out carburetter control adjustments and, if necessary, slow running adjustments, all as described previously. On models with automatic choke, check and if necessary top up and bleed the cooling system as described in **Chapter 4**.

2:9 Carburetter overhaul

Remove the carburetter as described in **Section 2:8**. Remove the top cover and service float and needle valve assemblies as described in **Section 2:7**. Remove the ancillary components and the internal jets from the carburetter body, but do not remove shafts and levers unless worn or damaged components are to be renewed. Note the positions of jets and mark shafts, levers and plate valves if they are to be removed, so that they can be reassembled in their correct relative positions. Use the correct size of screwdriver when removing jets, to avoid damage. Typical carburetter components are shown in **FIGS 2:11** and **2:12**. Specifications and jet sizes for the alternative types of carburetter which may be fitted are given in **Technical Data**. When removing idle adjustment screws, carefully count the number of turns taken to do so, then they or any replacement units fitted can be installed in the same positions to provide initial settings. This will facilitate later tuning and adjustment procedures.

Clean all parts in petrol or an approved carburetter cleaner, then examine them for wear or damage. Renew any faulty parts. Clean jets and passages thoroughly, using compressed air, clean petrol and a small brush. **Do not use cloth for cleaning purposes, as small fibres may remain after cleaning and clog the jets or passages. Never use a wire probe as this will damage or enlarge the jets.** If a jet has a blockage which cannot be cleared with compressed air, use a single bristle from a stiff brush for the purpose. If this method is unsuccessful, renew the jet. Carefully examine the tips of idle adjustment screws and renew if the tapered sealing surface is worn or damaged. Make sure that all sediment is cleared from the float chamber.

On completion, reassemble the carburetter in the reverse order of dismantling, using new gaskets throughout. Take care not to overtighten the jets or component fixing screws to avoid stripping the threads in the light alloy castings. Reassemble the carburetter top cover and make float level adjustments as described in **Section 2:7**. Refit the carburetter as described in **Section 2:8** and carry out linkage and slow running adjustments as described in **Section 2:7**.

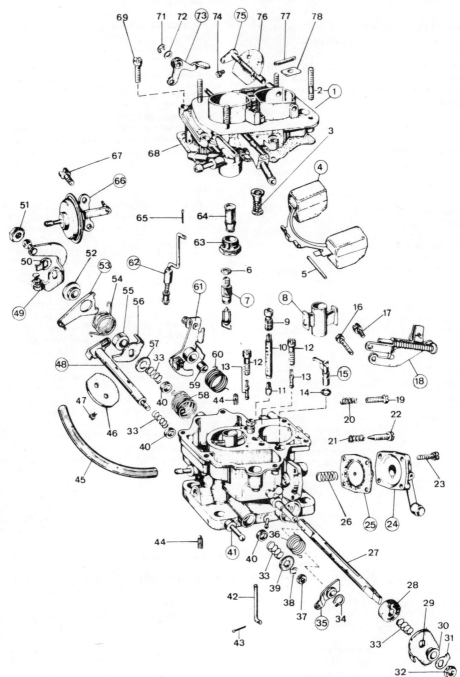

FIG 2:12   Typical carburetter components, Weber 32 DMTRA 200 shown

Key to Fig 2:12   1 Carburetter cover   2 Stud   3 Bowl vent valve   4 Float   5 Pin   6 Gasket   7 Needle valve   8 Venturi   9 Air metering jet   10 Emulsion tube   11 Main jet   12 Idle jet holders   13 Idle jets   14 Gasket   15 Accelerator pump nozzle   16, 17 Screws   18 Support   19 Idle screw   20, 21 Springs   22 Idle mixture screw   23 screw   24 Accelerator pump cover   25 Diaphragm   26 Spring   27 Throttle shaft, primary   28 Oil vapour distributor   29 Lever   30 Bushing   31 Lockwasher   32 Nut   33 Spring   34 Ring   35 Choke rod   36 Spring   37 Nut   38 Springwasher   39 Washer   40 Bushing   41 Carburetter body   42 Lever   43 Cotter pin   44 Secondary throttle stop screw   45 Hose   46 Throttle plate   47 Screw   48 Throttle shaft, secondary   49 Lever   50 Lockwasher   51 Nut   52 Bushing   53 Lever   54 Spring   55 Bushing   56 Primary shaft lever   57 Washer   58 Spring   59 Bushing   60 Spring   61 Lever   62 Rod   63 Filter plug   64 Filter   65 Cotter pin   66 Choke override   67 Screw   68 Cover gasket   69 Screw   71 Circlip   72 Washer   73 Choke over-ride control   74 Screw   75 Choke plate shaft   76 Choke plate   77 Clip   78 Dust cover

2:10 Emission control system

Models exported to the USA are equipped with a fuel evaporative emission control system to prevent fuel vapour from escaping into the atmosphere. The system incorporates a special three-way valve, a fuel liquid/vapour separator and an activated charcoal canister. The valve allows outside air to enter the fuel tank in order to vent the tank as fuel is used, but will not allow a reverse flow unless it is forced into the safety position by excessive pressure in the tank. Normal slight pressure increases in the fuel tank are compensated for as the valve operates to allow the tank to vent into the activated charcoal canister. The fuel vapour is then absorbed and stored until the engine is started, when the canister is purged through a hose connected to the engine inlet manifold, the vapour contents being drawn into the engine and burnt in the combustion chambers.

At the intervals recommended in the manufacturer's service schedule, the activated charcoal canister located in the engine compartment should be discarded and a new one fitted in its place. When removing the old unit, note the connections of hoses so that they can be correctly located on the new unit.

Apart from canister renewal, a general check on fuel evaporative emission control system components should be carried out, but this work should be entrusted to a fully equipped service station.

2:11 Fault diagnosis

(a) Leakage or insufficient fuel delivered

1 Air vent to tank restricted
2 Fuel pipe blocked
3 Air leaks at pipe connections
4 Fuel filter blocked

5 Pump gaskets faulty
6 Pump diaphragm defective
7 Pump valves sticking or seating badly

(b) Excessive fuel consumption

1 Carburetter requires adjustment
2 Fuel leakage
3 Sticking choke control
4 Float level too high
5 Dirty air cleaner
6 Worn jets in carburetter
7 Excessive engine temperature
8 Idling speed too high

(c) Idling speed too high

1 Rich fuel mixture
2 Throttle control sticking
3 Choke control sticking
4 Worn throttle valve

(d) Noisy fuel pump

1 Loose pump mountings
2 Air leaks on suction side of diaphragm
3 Obstruction in fuel pipeline
4 Clogged fuel filter

(e) No fuel delivery

1 Float needle valve stuck
2 Tank vent system blocked
3 Defective pump diaphragm
4 Pump valve stuck
5 Pipeline obstructed
6 Bad air leak on suction side of pump

NOTES

CHAPTER 3

THE IGNITION SYSTEM

3:1 Description

The ignition system is conventional, comprising an ignition coil, distributor and contact breaker assembly. The distributor incorporates automatic timing control by centrifugal mechanism and, on USA export models, a vacuum operated unit. As engine speed increases, the centrifugal action of rotating weights pivoting against the tension of small springs moves the contact breaker cam relative to the distributor drive shaft and progressively advances the ignition. On USA export models, the vacuum control unit is connected by small bore pipe to a fitting on the carburetter. At high degrees of vacuum the unit advances the ignition, but under load, at reduced vacuum, the unit progressively retards the ignition. On early models, the distributor is mounted in a horizontal position on the cylinder head and driven from the end of the camshaft. On later models, the distributor is mounted in a vertical position on the cylinder block and driven by the engine auxiliary shaft.

The ignition coil is wound as an auto-transformer with the primary and secondary windings connected in series, the common junction being connected to the contact breaker with the positive feed from the battery going to the opposite terminal of the LT windings via the ignition switch. When the contact breaker points are closed, current flows in the coil primary winding, magnetising the core and setting up a fairly strong magnetic field. Each time the contacts open, the battery current is cut off and the magnetic field collapses, inducing a high current in the primary winding and a high voltage in the secondary. The primary current is used to charge the capacitor connected across the contacts and the flow is high and virtually instantaneous. It is this high current peak which induces the surge in the secondary winding to produce the sparking voltage across the plug points. Without the capacitor the current peak would be much smaller and the sparking voltage considerably reduced, in fact to a point where it would be insufficient to fire the mixture in the engine cylinders. The capacitor, therefore, serves the dual purpose of minimising contact breaker points wear and providing the necessary high charging surge to ensure a powerful spark.

3:2 Routine maintenance

Pull off the two spring clips and remove the distributor cap. Refer to **FIG 3:1**. If a felt pad is fitted to the top of the distributor shaft as shown at 1, apply just sufficient engine oil to the pad to soak it. Apply a thin smear of grease to the

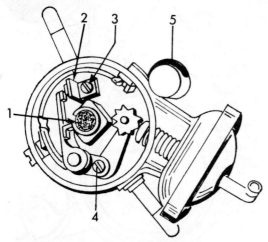

FIG 3:1   Upper components of typical distributor

four-sided cam which opens the contact points. Take great care to avoid oil or grease contaminating the contact breaker points 2, lubricating sparingly for this reason.

Adjusting the contact breaker points:

Turn the engine until one of the cams has opened the contact breaker points to their fullest extent, then check the gap between the points with clean feeler gauges. The correct gap is 0.37 to 0.43mm (0.015 to 0.017in). To adjust, loosen screw 3 and move the fixed contact point until the gap is correct. Tighten the screw and recheck the gap.

Cleaning the contact breaker points:

Use a fine carborundum stone or special contact point file to polish the points if they are dirty or pitted, taking care to keep the faces flat and square. If the points are too worn to clean up in this manner, they should be renewed. On completion of cleaning, wipe away all dust with a cloth moistened in petrol.

Renewing the contact breaker points:

Remove the screws shown at 3 and 4 in **FIG 3:1**, then disconnect the LT wiring and remove the points set. Wash the mating faces of the new contact points with methylated spirits to remove the protective coating, then install in the reverse order of removal. On completion, set the points gap as described previously.

Checking rotor arm:

Check the rotor arm for cracks and for excessive wear or burning of the brass contact strip. Renew the arm if any faults are found. To check rotor insulation, remove the central HT lead from the distributor cap and hold it about half an inch from the brass strip on the rotor. To avoid shocks, hold the lead well away from the end. With the ignition switched on, flick open the contact points. If a spark jumps the gap the rotor is faulty and must be renewed.

3:3 Ignition faults

If the engine runs unevenly, set it to idle at approximately 1000rev/min and, taking care not to touch any conducting part of the sparking plug leads, remove and replace each lead from its plug in turn. To avoid shocks during this operation it is necessary to wear a thick glove or to use insulated pliers. Doing this to a plug which is firing correctly will accentuate uneven running but will make no difference if the plug is not firing.

Having by this means located the faulty cylinder, stop the engine and remove the plug lead. Pull back the insulation or remove the connectors so that the end of the lead is exposed. Alternatively, use an extension piece, such as a small bar or drill, pushed into the plug connector. Hold the lead carefully to avoid shocks, so that the end is about $\frac{1}{8}$in away from the cylinder head. Crank the engine with the starter. A strong, regular spark confirms that the fault lies with the sparking plug which should be removed and cleaned as described in **Section 3:6**, or renewed if defective.

If the spark is weak and irregular, check the condition of the lead and, if it is perished or cracked, renew it and repeat the test. If no improvement results, check that the inside of the distributor cap is clean and dry and that there is no sign of tracking, which can be seen as a thin black line between the electrodes or to some metal part in contact with the cap. Tracking can only be cured by fitting a new cap. Check that the carbon brush in the cap is in good condition and free to move in and out against its internal spring. Check the brass segments inside the cap for wear or burning. Renew the cap if any fault is found.

If these checks do not cure a weak HT spark, or if no spark can be obtained at the plug or lead, check the LT circuit as described next.

Testing the low tension circuit:

Check that the contact breaker points are clean and correctly set, then proceed as follows:

Remove the sparking plugs. Disconnect the thin wire from the coil that leads to the distributor. Connect a 12 volt test lamp between these terminals, switch on the ignition and turn the engine slowly by pulling on the alternator drive belt or by using a spanner on the crankshaft pulley nut. If the lamp lights and goes out as the points close and open, the circuit is in order. If the lamp fails to light, there is a fault in the LT circuit.

Remove the lamp and connect the wire to the coil and distributor. If the fault lies in the LT circuit, use the lamp to carry out the following tests with the ignition switched on. Remove the wire from the ignition switch side of the coil and connect the lamp between the end of this wire and earth. If the lamp fails to light, it indicates a fault in the wiring between the battery and the coil or in the ignition switch. Reconnect the wire if the lamp lights.

Disconnect the wire from the coil that connects to the distributor. Connect the lamp between the coil terminal and earth. If the lamp fails to light it indicates a fault in the coil primary winding and a new coil must be fitted. Reconnect the wire if the lamp lights and disconnect its other end from the distributor. If the lamp does not light when connected between the end of this wire and earth, it indicates a fault in the section of wire.

Capacitor:

The best method of testing a capacitor (condenser) is by substitution. Disconnect the original capacitor and connect a new one between the LT terminal on the distributor and earth for test purposes. The capacitor is shown at 5 in **FIG 3:1**. If a new capacitor is proved to be required, it can then be properly fitted. The capacitor is of 0.22 to 0.23 microfarad capacity.

3:4 Removing and dismantling distributor

Removal:

Turn the engine until No 1 cylinder is at TDC on the firing stroke. Number 1 is the cylinder nearest the timing gear end of the engine. To do this, remove the distributor cap and turn the engine until the rotor points towards the cap segment for No 1 cylinder, or turn the engine until both valves in No 1 cylinder are closed, removing the camshaft cover to view the cam lobes (see **Chapter 1**). This done, turn the engine a little more as necessary until the timing notch in the crankshaft pulley aligns with the 10° advance mark on the front of the timing gear cover for European models, or with the TDC mark for USA export models (see **FIG 3:2**).

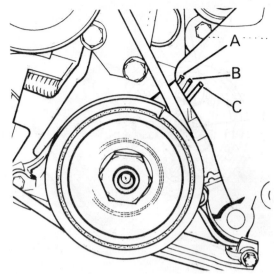

FIG 3:2 The ignition timing marks
Key to Fig 3:2   A 10°   B 5°   C 0°

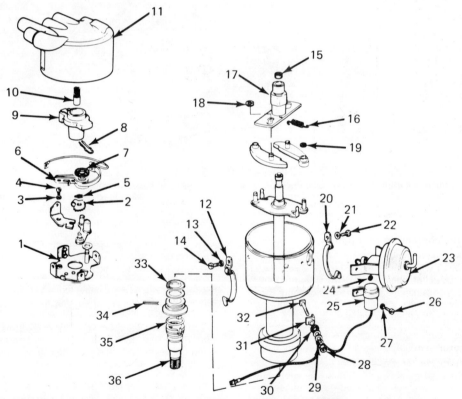

FIG 3:3   Distributor components, first type

Key to Fig 3:3   1 Contact breaker plate   2 Star gear   3 Washer   4 Screw   5 Clip   6 Contact breaker points   7 Washer
8 Clip   9 Rotor arm   10 Spring contact   11 Cap   12 Clip   13 Washer   14 Screw   15 Rubber ring   16 Spring
17 Cam   18 Circlip   19 Washer   20 Clip   21 Washer   22 Screw   23 Vacuum unit   24 Washer   25 Capacitor
26 Screw   27 Washer   28 Nut   29 Lockwasher   30 Fibre washer   31 Terminal   32 Bolt   33 Washer   34 Pin
35 Seal   36 Gear

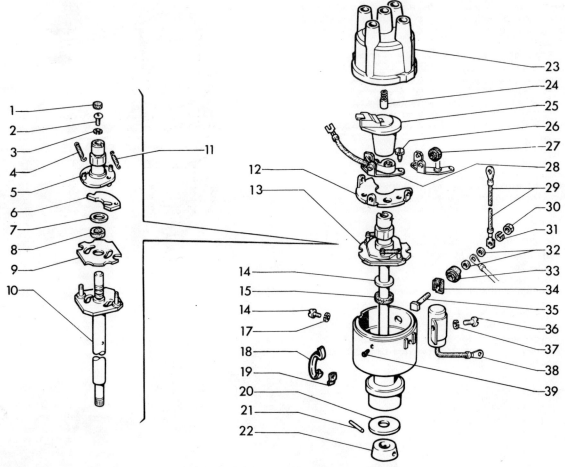

FIG 3:4 Distributor components, second type

Key to Fig 3:4   1 Felt pad   2 Screw   3 Washer   4 Spring   5 Cam assembly   6 Advance weight   7 Washer
8 Insulator   9 Advance mechanism plate   10 Shaft assembly   11 Spring   12 Contact breaker plate   13 Centrifugal advance
mechanism   14 Washer   15 Insulator   16 Screw   17 Washer   18 Spring clip   19 Hinge   20 Washer   21 Pin
22 Collar   23 Distributor cap   24 Carbon brush   25 Rotor arm   26 Lockscrew   27 Insulator   28 Contact breaker
29 LT lead   30 Terminal nut   31, 32 Washers   33, 34 Insulators   35 Terminal bolt   36 Screw   37 Washer   38 Capacitor
39 Screw

With the distributor cap removed, disconnect the low tension wiring from the distributor. Note the position of the rotor relative to the distributor body and mark the position of the distributor body relative to the engine block or cylinder head. Release the clamp securing distributor in position, then pull the distributor from its mounting. Distributor installation will be facilitated if the engine is not turned while the distributor is removed.

Refitting:

With the timing marks aligned correctly as previously described, offer the distributor into position with the mark on the body aligned with the mark on block or head. Turn the rotor to the position noted during removal and push the distributor fully into place, noting that the rotor may have

to be turned a fraction to allow the drive mechanism to engage correctly. When the distributor seats the rotor must be pointing towards the cap segment for firing No 1 cylinder. Temporarily tighten the clamp to secure the distributor, then check the ignition timing as described in **Section 3:5**.

Dismantling:

Pull the rotor from the distributor shaft, then remove the contact breaker points as described in **Section 3:2**. Refer to **FIG 3:3** or **3:4** according to the type of distributor fitted.

If a vacuum unit is installed, remove the fixing screws and detach the unit from the contact breaker plate. Use a suitable punch to remove the retaining pin, then remove the drive gear and washers. Pull the distributor shaft with upper components from the distributor body and dismantle into the order shown in the illustration if necessary.

Thoroughly clean all parts in petrol or other suitable solvent and dry them. Examine for wear or damage and renew parts as necessary. Service the contact breaker points as described in **Section 3:2**.

After inspection and servicing, reassemble the distributor in the reverse order of dismantling. Lightly lubricate the shaft bearings with engine oil and the centrifugal advance mechanism with grease. Lubricate upper distributor components and set contact points gap as described in **Section 3:2**. Check that the centrifugal advance mechanism operates by holding the shaft while turning the rotor to the limit of its travel. When released, the rotor should snap back to its original position.

3:5 Timing the ignition

The piston for No 1 cylinder must be at TDC on the compression stroke. To check this, either remove the rocker cover and check that both cam lobes are pointing away from tappets for No 1 cylinder (see **Chapter 1**), or by removing No 1 sparking plug and turning the engine forwards until compression can be felt by a thumb placed over the plughole. This done, turn the engine a little more as necessary to correctly align the timing marks as described in **Section 3:4**. **Do not turn the engine backwards.**

Electrical setting:

With the engine correctly set as previously described, connect a 12 volt test lamp in parallel with the contact breaker points. One lead will go to the terminal on the side of the distributor and one to earth. Slacken the distributor clamp bolt just enough to allow the distributor body to be turned by hand. Switch on the ignition and ensure that the contact points are fully closed, turning the distributor body to ensure this. Now turn the distributor body very slowly until the lamp just lights, which indicates that the points are beginning to open. Tighten the clamp bolt at this point and confirm the accuracy of the setting by turning the engine and checking that the test lamp lights up again exactly as the notch in the crankshaft pulley lines up with the appropriate timing mark on the front cover. It is recommended that the setting be checked for accuracy using stroboscopic equipment as described next.

Stroboscopic timing:

If a stroboscopic timing lamp is available a more accurate setting can be obtained with the engine running at idling speed. Note that the engine must be at normal operating temperature and idling at a speed of 850 rev/min. Adjust idle speed if necessary as described in **Chapter 2**. The procedure will be facilitated if the appropriate timing mark and the notch in the crankshaft pulley are marked with dabs of white paint.

Connect the stroboscopic lamp equipment according to the manufacturer's instructions, into the ignition circuit for No 1 cylinder. Start the engine and allow it to idle at the correct speed, then aim the stroboscopic lamp at the

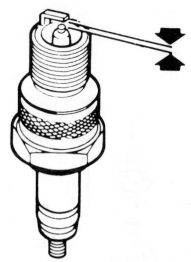

FIG 3:5   Checking sparking plug points gap

timing marks. If the marks do not appear correctly in alignment, slacken the distributor clamp bolt slightly and rotate the distributor body until timing is correct, then retighten the bolt. Switch off the ignition and remove the stroboscopic equipment, then check engine idle speed as described in **Chapter 2**.

3:6 Sparking plugs

Sparking plugs should be of the recommended type, details of which are given in **Technical Data**. The gaps should be set to 0.5 to 0.6mm (0.020 to 0.024in) by bending the outer electrode only (see **FIG 3:5**). Have sparking plugs cleaned on an abrasive-blasting machine and tested under pressure with the electrode gaps correctly set. Any plug which fails the test should be renewed. As a general rule, plugs should be cleaned and tested at about 6000 mile intervals and renewed at about 12,000 mile intervals, or before if badly worn.

Sparking plug leads:

Renew HT leads if they are defective in any way. Inspect for broken, swollen or deteriorated insulation which can be the cause of current leakage, especially in wet weather conditions. Also check the condition of the plug connectors at the ends of the leads.

3:7 Fault diagnosis

(a) Engine will not fire

1 Battery discharged
2 Contact breaker points dirty, pitted or maladjusted
3 Distributor cap dirty, cracked or tracking
4 Brush inside distributor cap not touching rotor
5 Faulty cable or loose connection in LT circuit
6 Distributor rotor arm cracked
7 Faulty coil
8 Broken contact breaker spring
9 Contact points stuck open

(b) Engine misfires

1 Check 2, 3, 5 and 7 in (a)
2 Weak contact breaker spring
3 HT plug or coil lead cracked or perished
4 Loose sparking plug
5 Sparking plug insulation cracked
6 Sparking plug gap incorrect
7 Ignition timing too far advanced

(c) Poor acceleration

1 Ignition retarded
2 Centrifugal advance weights seized
3 Centrifugal advance springs weak, broken or disconnected
4 Loose distributor mounting
5 Excessive contact points gap
6 Worn sparking plugs
7 Faulty vacuum unit or leaking pipe

CHAPTER 4

THE COOLING SYSTEM

4:1 Description

The cooling system is pressurised and thermostatically controlled, using a corrugated fin type radiator located at the front of the car. The radiator is connected to the engine cooling system by means of pipes and hoses routed beneath the car. Water circulation is assisted by a centrifugal pump which is mounted on the engine cylinder block. The cooling fan, powered by an electric motor, is mounted in a shroud attached to the radiator and controlled by a thermoswitch.

The water pump, together with the alternator, is driven by means of a belt from the crankshaft pulley. The water pump takes coolant from the bottom of the radiator and delivers it to the cylinder block from which it rises to the cylinder head. At normal operating temperatures the thermostat is open and the coolant returns to the top of the radiator. At lower temperatures, the thermostat is closed and the coolant bypasses the radiator and returns directly to the pump inlet. This provides a rapid warm up and good heater performance.

An expansion tank containing a quantity of coolant is connected to the main system by means of a hose. At high operating temperatures, when the coolant in the system expands, excess coolant passes through a valve into the expansion tank. When the system cools, the valve allows coolant from the tank to flow back into the system. With this system, no coolant loss should occur during normal operation.

4:2 Routine maintenance

Apart from an occasional check on the condition of the hoses and hose clips and a visual check on coolant level in the expansion tank, very little maintenance should be necessary. There should also be no need for regular topping up of the coolant. If topping up is required frequently, the system should be examined for leaks before adding coolant.

Check the level of coolant in the expansion tank and top up as required. The expansion tank should be filled to a point approximately 3.0in above the 'MIN' mark. The level will be higher when the engine is hot. If it is essential to remove the expansion tank cap when the engine is hot, hold the cap with a large piece of rag. Turn the cap anticlockwise to the safety stop and wait a few moments for pressure to be released before lifting off the cap.

It is recommended that a solution containing antifreeze formulated for use in aluminium engines is maintained in the system all year round. Topping up should therefore be

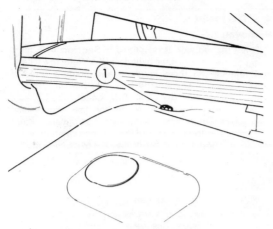

FIG 4:1   Radiator bleed screw 1

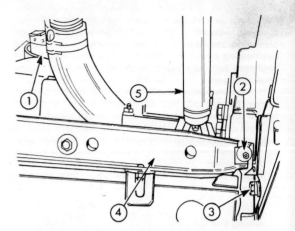

FIG 4:2   Radiator removal

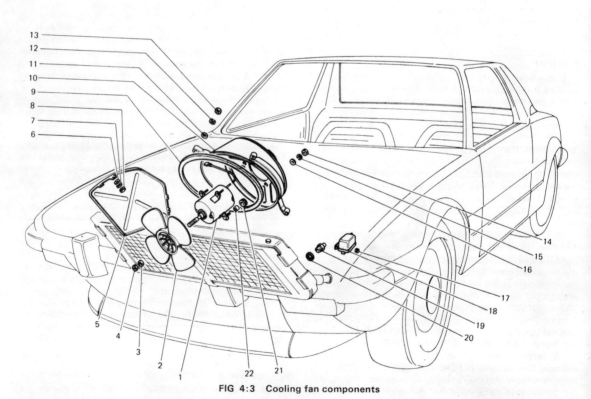

FIG 4:3   Cooling fan components

Key to Fig 4:3   1 Fan motor   2 Fan   3 Washer   4 Nut   5 Plate   6 Washer   7 Lockwasher   8 Nut   9 Gasket   10 Shroud   11 Washer   12 Lockwasher   13 Nut   14 Nut   15 Lockwasher   16 Washer   17 Nut   18 Relay   19 Thermoswitch   20 Gasket   21 Lockring   22 Spacer

carried out with the correct mixture of antifreeze and water to avoid weakening the solution in use. Apart from protecting the system against freezing in winter and overheating in summer, the inhibitors contained in the antifreeze help to prevent corrosion and scaling of the cooling system.

It is recommended that at yearly intervals the cooling system be drained, flushed to remove sediment then refilled with fresh antifreeze mixture. Check that the clips are tight on all hoses and that the expansion tank cap and radiator cap are in good condition and sealing effectively. Loss of system pressure due to a leaking cap can be a cause of overheating.

Regular checks should be made on drive belt condition and tension as described in **Section 4:5**.

Draining the system:

This work must only be carried out when the engine is cool. If the system is being drained for a change of coolant, the old coolant should be discarded, but if drained to allow for other servicing operations to be carried out the coolant should be collected in a clean container for re-use.

Remove the expansion tank cap and the radiator cap. Open the drain tap at the bottom of the radiator or, if no drain tap is fitted, slacken the hose clip and detach the bottom hose from the radiator. Disconnect the expansion tank hose at the radiator and drain the contents of the tank. Open the tap located on the alternator side of the engine to drain the cylinder block.

Flushing:

Use a hose to run clean water in through the radiator filler till it runs clean at the drain points. Close the drain points and fill the system through the radiator filler. Start the engine and run for long enough to allow normal operating temperature to be reached, this being when the top radiator hose feels warm to the touch. Stop the engine and repeat the draining procedure again before any sediment has time to settle. If necessary, repeat the operation. Always allow the system to cool before filling. Do not add cold water to the cooling system when the engine is hot, otherwise there is the danger of cracking the cylinder block.

Filling:

Make sure that the drain points are closed, that all hoses are properly connected and that the heater controls are in the maximum heat position. Completely fill the radiator then fill the expansion tank to a point approximately 3.0in above the 'MIN' mark. Start the engine and allow it to idle. Open the front luggage compartment lid and locate the radiator bleed screw which is shown at 1 in **FIG 4:1**. Open the bleed screw while the engine is idling and close it firmly again when coolant flows through without air bubbles. Top up again to the correct level in the expansion tank, make sure that the radiator and expansion tank caps are firmly in place, then allow the engine to run until normal operating temperature is reached. Switch off, allow the system to cool down fully, then recheck and if necessary top up level in expansion tank.

4:3 The radiator
Removal:

Drain the radiator as described in **Section 4:2**, there being no need to drain the cylinder block. Refer to **FIG 4:2** and remove the three lower screws holding grille to crossmember 4. Loosen the four nuts holding plate to body, then remove the plate. Disconnect hoses 5 from radiator. Disconnect the wiring for fan unit 1 and disconnect wiring from thermoswitch at radiator. Raise and safely support the front of the car, then carefully lower the radiator from the car, taking care not to damage the fan unit.

Refitting:

This is a reversal of the removal procedure. Make sure that all hose connections are secure, then refill and bleed the cooling system as described in **Section 4:2**.

4:4 The cooling fan

The cooling fan is electrically operated and switched on and off, according to coolant temperature, by a thermoswitch attached to the radiator. The layout of the system is shown in **FIG 4:3**.

If the fan operates when the cooling system is cold, the thermoswitch is faulty or there is a short circuit in the fan wiring. If the fan does not operate at all, check fuse number L-10, then check that the motor is in order by connecting jumper leads from the battery to the motor terminals. If the motor is in order, check the thermoswitch by removing the two leads from the switch and connecting them together then turning on the ignition. If the fan then operates, the thermoswitch is faulty. If the switch is in order, disconnect wires from terminals 30/51 and 87 on the relay and connect these wires together. If the fan then runs, it indicates either a faulty fan relay or no current supply to the relay. Check current supply to relay by disconnecting the wire from terminal 86 on the relay and connecting a 12 volt test lamp between the end of this wire and earth with the ignition switched on. If the lamp lights, the wiring is in order and the relay must be at fault.

If the fan motor or any operating components in the circuit are faulty, the component in question must be renewed complete. Note that the thermoswitch should switch on and cause the fan to cut in at a temperature of approximately 90°C (194°F) and switch off when the temperature drops to approximately 85°C (185°F). The thermoswitch can be removed from the radiator after disconnecting the wiring, then a new unit fitted complete with new gasket. As a small amount of coolant will be lost during this operation, top up and bleed the system afterwards as described in **Section 4:2**. Removal of the cooling fan, motor and shroud are straightforward operations, but disconnect the battery earth cable before disconnecting fan circuit wiring.

4:5 Drive belt tensioning

It is important to maintain the correct tension of the alternator and water pump drive belt as a tight belt will cause undue wear on the pulleys and component bearings. Conversely, a slack belt will slip and, possibly, cause

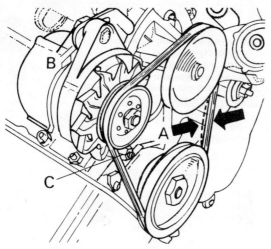

FIG 4:4   Drive belt tensioning

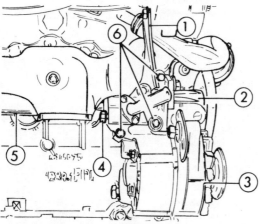

FIG 4:5   Water pump removal

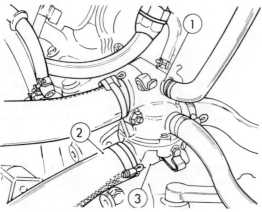

FIG 4:6   Thermostat removal

decreased output from the driven components. If the belt is worn, damaged or oil contaminated it must be renewed.

Tension is correct when the belt can be deflected by 10 to 15mm (0.4 to 0.6in) when firm hand pressure is applied at the points arrowed at **A** in **FIG 4:4**. If adjustment is necessary, slacken the alternator mounting bolts **B** and **C** then pivot the alternator away from the engine until belt tension is correct. If a lever is used to move the alternator, it must be applied to the mounting bracket only, never to the alternator body. Hold the alternator in position while tightening the mounting bolts. The belt can be removed by slackening the bolts, swinging the alternator towards the engine then removing the belt over the pulleys. Fit the new belt over the pulleys then set to the correct tension. The tension of a new belt should be checked after driving for a few miles, then readjusted if necessary to take up the initial stretch.

4:6 The water pump
Removal:

Drain the cooling system as described in **Section 4:2**. Remove the protective panels from bottom righthand side of engine. Remove the drive belt as described in **Section 4:5**, then refer to **FIG 4:5**.

Disconnect the wiring from the rear of alternator 3, then remove the mounting bolts and detach the alternator. Disconnect hoses from water pump 2. Remove the three nuts and washers 4 securing pipe 5 to pump. On models with emission control system, remove bolt securing air pump support 1 to water pump. Remove the four bolts 6 securing water pump to engine, then remove the pump. Remove and discard the gasket.

If the water pump is internally defective it is possible for repairs to be carried out, but as the work requires the use of special tools and press equipment it should be carried out by a fully equipped service station.

Refitting:

This is a reversal of the removal procedure, using a new gasket. On completion, set drive belt tension as described in **Section 4:5** then fill and bleed cooling system as described in **Section 4:2**.

4:7 The thermostat
Removal:

Drain sufficient coolant as described in **Section 4:2** to bring the level below that of the thermostat housing. Remove the air cleaner assembly as described in **Chapter 2**. Refer to **FIG 4:6** and disconnect hose 2. Remove the three bolts and washers securing cover 3 to union 1, then remove the thermostat and gaskets.

Testing:

Clean the thermostat and immerse it in a container of cold water together with a zero to 100°C thermometer. Heat the water, keeping it stirred, and check that the valve opens at between 73 and 77°C. The valve should be fully open at approximately 90°C. The valve should close tightly when the thermostat is removed from the hot water and placed in cold water. If the thermostat operates correctly it may be refitted, but if not it must be renewed.

Refitting:

This is a reversal of the removal procedure, using new gaskets. On completion, fill and bleed the cooling system as described in **Section 4:2**.

4:8 Frost precautions

With the correct coolant solution in use as described in **Section 4:2**, no additional frost precautions should be necessary. However, it is advisable to have the solution tested at intervals during the winter to make certain that it has not weakened. A hydrometer calibrated to read both specific gravity and temperature for the type of coolant in the system must be used, most garages having such equipment. Always ensure that the antifreeze mixture used for filling the system is of sufficient strength to provide protection against freezing, according to the manufacturer's instructions.

4:9 Fault diagnosis

(a) Internal coolant leakage

1 Cracked cylinder wall
2 Loose cylinder head bolts or nuts
3 Cracked cylinder head
4 Faulty head gasket

(b) Poor circulation

1 Radiator blocked
2 Engine water passages restricted
3 Low coolant level
4 Slack pump drive belt
5 Defective thermostat
6 Perished or collapsed radiator hoses
7 Faulty water pump

(c) Corrosion

1 Impurities in the coolant
2 Infrequent draining and flushing

(d) Overheating

1 Check (b)
2 Sludge in crankcase
3 Faulty ignition timing
4 Low oil level in engine sump
5 Tight engine
6 Choked exhaust system
7 Binding brakes
8 Slipping clutch
9 Incorrect valve timing
10 Mixture too weak
11 Faulty fan motor, relay or thermoswitch

NOTES

CHAPTER 5

THE CLUTCH

5:1 Description
5:2 Clutch adjustment
5:3 Removing and dismantling clutch

5:4 Assembling and refitting clutch
5:5 Servicing hydraulic system
5:6 Fault diagnosis

5:1 Description

A single dry plate clutch of diaphragm spring type is fitted, the main components being the driven plate, pressure plate assembly and release bearing.

The driven plate consists of a resilient steel disc attached to a hub which slides on the splined gearbox input shaft. The pressure plate assembly consists of the pressure plate, diaphragm spring and cover, this cover being attached to the outer face of the engine flywheel. The release bearing is a ballbearing of special construction with an elongated outer ring that presses directly against the diaphragm spring when the clutch pedal is operated.

The clutch operating mechanism is hydraulic, the clutch pedal actuating a master cylinder where pressure on the fluid is generated, this pressure being transmitted through a hose to a clutch slave cylinder mounted on the clutch housing. Slave cylinder action is transmitted to the release bearing by a lever.

When the clutch is fully engaged, the driven plate is nipped between the pressure plate and the flywheel and transmits torque to the gearbox by turning the splined input shaft. When the clutch pedal is depressed the pressure plate is withdrawn from the driven plate by hydraulic pressure, the driven plate then ceasing to transmit torque.

Adjustment of the clutch operating mechanism should be carried out when necessary to compensate for the normal wear of driven plate friction linings.

5:2 Clutch adjustment

Clutch pedal travel:

Total travel of the clutch pedal from the stop on the pedal bracket to the floor of the car should be approximately 170mm (6.7in). If incorrect, refer to **FIG 5:1** and loosen locknut 1. Turn adjustment screw 2 until travel of pedal 3 is correct, then firmly tighten locknut 1.

Pedal free play:

Operate the clutch pedal gently by hand to determine the amount of free play before pressure can be felt. This should be approximately 28.5mm (1.25in). If incorrect, locate the adjustment mechanism at slave cylinder 2 as shown in **FIG 5:2**. Slacken the locknut 9 on pushrod which operates release lever 1, then adjust the length of pushrod to alter pedal free play, checking between each adjustment. When correct, tighten the locknut firmly, operate the clutch pedal fully several times, then recheck the adjustment. Finally, recheck the adjustment after road testing the car.

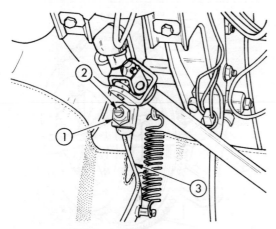

FIG 5:1   Pedal travel adjustment

5:3 Removing and dismantling clutch

Remove the gearbox as described in **Chapter 6**. Refer to **FIG 5:3**. Mark the clutch cover and engine flywheel as shown at 1, so that the clutch cover can be refitted in its original position to preserve the balance of the assembly. Slacken the bolts securing clutch cover to flywheel alternately and evenly until all spring pressure is released. Remove the bolts and lift off the clutch pressure plate assembly and driven disc, taking care not to get grease or oil on the friction linings.

If the release bearing is to be removed from the clutch housing, refer to **FIG 5:4**. Remove spring clips 5 securing release bearing carrier to operating lever and remove the bearing assembly. If the lever assembly is to be removed, remove bolt 11 and washer 12, then pull lever 1 out of the fork and clutch housing.

Servicing:

The clutch cover, pressure plate and diaphragm spring assembly must not be dismantled. If any part is faulty the assembly must be renewed complete.

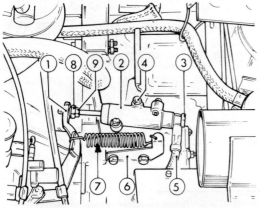

FIG 5:2   Slave cylinder installation

Key to Fig 5:2   1 Engagement lever   2 Slave cylinder
3 Union   4 Bolt   5 Hose   6 Bracket   7 Return spring
8, 9 Adjustment nuts

Inspect the surfaces of the flywheel where the driven plate makes contact. Small scratches on the surface are unimportant, but if there are deep scratches the flywheel must be machined smooth or renewed. Check the pressure plate for scoring or damage and check that the working surface is flat and true, using a metal straightedge. Make the check at several points. Check the diaphragm spring for cracks or other damage and the clutch cover for damage or distortion.

Check the release bearing for roughness when it is pressed and turned by hand. Clean the bearing by wiping with a cloth only. Do not use solvents for cleaning purposes as they would wash the internal lubricant from the bearing. If the engagement lever has been removed from the clutch housing, check the components for wear or damage, paying particular attention to bearing bush 9 and 'O' ring 8. It is recommended that the latter be renewed whenever the components are dismantled. Note that the bush and the bore in the bearing carrier should be lightly greased during reassembly.

Check the driven plate for loose rivets and broken or very loose torsional springs. Check the plate for distortion. Slight distortion can often be cured by installing the plate on the gearbox input shaft splines and twisting the plate by hand. If not, the plate should be renewed, as distortion can cause rapid wear and operational faults. Friction linings should be well proud of the rivets and have a polished glaze through which the grain of the material is clearly visible. A dark, glazed deposit indicates oil on the facings and, as this condition cannot be rectified, a new or relined plate will be required. Any sign of oil in the clutch indicates leakage from the engine or gearbox and the cause must be traced and rectified. Check the splines in the driven plate hub and on the gearbox input shaft, removing any burrs or, if there are signs of heavy wear, renewing parts as necessary.

It is not recommended that owners attempt to reline the clutch driven plate themselves, as the linings must be fitted and trued on the disc and the whole checked under a press. For this reason, the driven plate should be relined at a service station or an exchange unit obtained and fitted.

5:4 Assembling and refitting clutch

When the clutch assembly is refitted to the engine flywheel, it must be centralised before tightening down, using tool A.70210, a universal clutch alignment tool or a spare gearbox input shaft, as shown at 3 in **FIG 5:3**.

Fit the tool through the pressure plate and driven plate then offer the assembly to the flywheel, engaging the ends of the tool in the pilot bearing at the end of the crankshaft. Note that the protruding side of driven plate hub must face away from the engine flywheel. Index the alignment marks on cover and flywheel which were made previously, then fit the retaining bolts fingertight. Tighten the bolts alternately and evenly to a final torque of 1.5kgm (11lb ft).

Refit the release bearing and engagement lever mechanism in the reverse order of removal. Make sure that the 'O' ring is installed on the shaft, then press the shaft down into transmission and through operating fork. Continue pressing down until the shaft engages in the transmission boss, then align the fork and fit and tighten the locking bolt and washer.

Remove the alignment tool from the clutch assembly, then refit the gearbox as described in **Chapter 6**.

5:5 Servicing hydraulic system

At regular intervals the level of fluid in the clutch master cylinder reservoir, shown at 1 in **FIG 5:5**, should be checked. If necessary, fluid must be added to bring the level up to the neck of the reservoir. Wipe dirt from around the cap before removing it and make sure that the vent hole is clear before refitting. The same fluid should be used as recommended for the braking system in **Chapter 10**.

Master cylinder:

Removal:

Refer to **Chapter 9** and remove the steering column. Refer to **FIG 5:5**. Place suitable rags beneath the master cylinder assembly to catch any fluid spillage, noting that fluid is poisonous and that it can damage paintwork. Release clip 4 and release hose 2 from master cylinder connection, immediately plugging the hose to prevent leakage. Disconnect and plug pipe 3. Remove the two bolts and washers 6 securing master cylinder to bracket 5, then remove cylinder by pulling away from pushrod 8.

Dismantling:

Refer to **FIG 5:6**. Remove dust boot 3, then remove circlip 1. Remove the remaining components from cylinder bore, using a compressed air nozzle or tyre pump at the fluid outlet hole if removal proves difficult. Remove lockplate 6 and connector 5 with seal 4.

Discard all rubber seals and the rubber boot and obtain new parts to replace them. Wash all remaining parts in the correct grade of brake fluid or methylated spirits only. Examine the parts and renew any found to be worn or damaged. Check the piston and cylinder bore for scoring, damage or corrosion and renew if any fault is found. Ensure that the inlet port from the reservoir and the outlet port to the pipe union are clear.

Reassembly:

Observe absolute cleanliness during assembly to prevent oil or dirt from contacting the parts. Dip all internal components in clean approved brake fluid and assemble them wet. Use the fingers only to enter the seals in the bore to prevent damage. Press the piston assembly down the cylinder bore against the spring and hold in position while installing the circlip. Fit the new rubber boot.

Installation:

This is a reversal of the removal procedure, using a new clip to secure fluid supply hose to connector on master cylinder. Refit steering column as described in **Chapter 9**. On completion, bleed the system as described later then carry out adjustment procedures described in **Section 5:2**.

Slave cylinder:

Removal:

Refer to **FIG 5:2**. If the cylinder is to be removed for overhaul, unscrew union 3 and remove fluid hose 5, plugging or taping the ends to prevent leakage. If the cylinder is to be removed for access to other components only, leave the hose connected and support the cylinder by

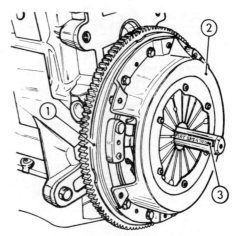

FIG 5:3   Clutch assembly installation

suitable means after removal to prevent strain on the hose. In this case, the system will not require bleeding when the cylinder is refitted, but note that the clutch pedal must not be touched while the cylinder is removed.

Remove the splitpin retaining pushrod to engagement lever 1. Open the bleed screw to allow the pushrod to retract, then disconnect spring 7 and close the bleed screw. Push the engagement lever away from the cylinder, then remove the two bolts and washers 4 securing cylinder to support plate 6. Pull the cylinder away from the support plate.

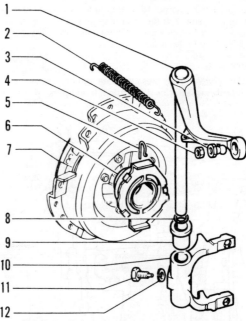

FIG 5:4   Release mechanism components

Key to Fig 5:4   1 Engagement lever and shaft   2 Return spring   3 Adjustment nut   4 Locknut   5 Spring clip
6 Carrier   7 Clutch assembly   8 'O' ring   9 Bush
10 Fork   11 Lock bolt   12 Washer

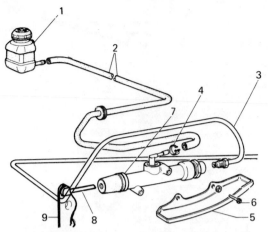

FIG 5:5   Master cylinder installation

Key to Fig 5:5   1 Fluid reservoir   2 Supply hose   3 Pipe
4 Clip   5 Bracket   6 Bolt   7 Master cylinder   8 Pushrod
9 Clutch pedal

Dismantling:

Refer to **FIG 5:7**. Remove pushrod and boot 7, then remove internal components from cylinder using compressed air or a tyre pump at the fluid outlet hole if removal proves difficult. Remove bleed screw 5. Service the internal components in the manner described previously for the master cylinder assembly.

Installation:

This is a reversal of the removal procedure, holding the engagement lever against spring pressure while installing and tightening the retaining bolts. If the fluid hose was disconnected from slave cylinder, reconnect using new gaskets then bleed the system as described next. In all cases, finally adjust clutch mechanism as described in **Section 5:2**.

Bleeding the system:

This operation is necessary to remove any air which may have entered the system, due to the removal of components, or if the fluid level in the reservoir has been allowed to drop too low and air has entered through the fluid supply passage.

A need for bleeding can be indicated if the clutch drags and cannot be fully released with the pedal pushed to the floor.

Make sure that the fluid level in the reservoir is correct, topping up if necessary. Locate the bleed screw on the slave cylinder, then remove the rubber dust cap if fitted. Attach a length of rubber or plastic tubing to the bleed screw and lead the free end of the tube into a clean glass jar, into which sufficient fluid of the correct type has been added to cover the end of the tube.

Unscrew the bleed screw by about three-quarters of a turn. Have an assistant depress the clutch pedal fully to the floor, then pause for a moment before allowing the pedal to return gently. Continue this action and watch the stream of fluid being pumped into the jar. When no air bubbles can be seen, hold the pedal at the end of a downstroke and

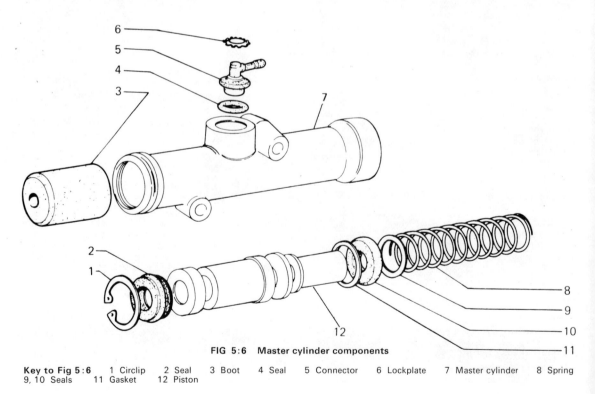

FIG 5:6   Master cylinder components

Key to Fig 5:6   1 Circlip   2 Seal   3 Boot   4 Seal   5 Connector   6 Lockplate   7 Master cylinder   8 Spring
9, 10 Seals   11 Gasket   12 Piston

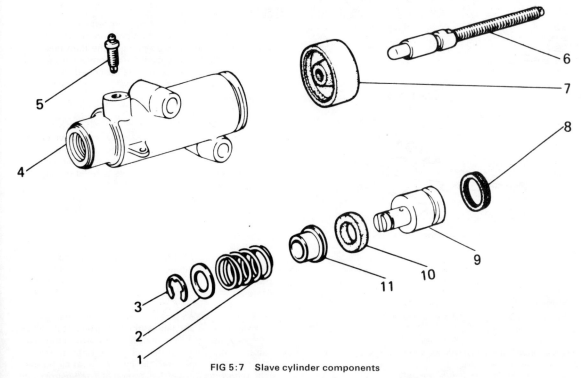

FIG 5:7 Slave cylinder components

Key to Fig 5:7   1 Spring   2 Washer   3 Retaining clip   4 Slave cylinder   5 Bleed screw   6 Pushrod   7 Boot
8 Seal   9 Piston   10 Seal   11 Bush

tighten the bleed screw. Replenish the fluid in the reservoir frequently during this operation. If the level falls too low, air may be drawn into the system and the operation will have to be restarted.

On completion, top up the fluid to the correct level and check clutch mechanism adjustment as described in **Section 5:2**. It is not advisable to re-use fluid drained from the system unless it is new and perfectly clean. If so, allow it to stand for at least 24 hours before re-use to ensure that it is free from air bubbles. Always store the fluid in sealed containers to prevent dirt or moisture contamination.

5:6 Fault diagnosis

(a) Drag or spin

1 Oil or grease on driven plate linings
2 Misalignment between engine and splined shaft
3 Driven plate hub binding on splined shaft
4 Distorted driven plate
5 Warped or damaged pressure plate or clutch cover
6 Broken driven plate linings
7 Dirt or foreign matter in clutch
8 Air in hydraulic system
9 Clutch adjustment incorrect

(b) Fierceness or snatch

1 Check 1, 2, 3 and 9 in (a)
2 Worn driven plate linings

(c) Slip

1 Check 1, 2 and 9 in (a)
2 Worn driven plate linings
3 Weak diaphragm spring
4 Seized piston in master or slave cylinder

(d) Judder

1 Check 1 and 2 in (a)
2 Pressure plate not parallel with flywheel face
3 Contact area of driven plate linings unevenly worn
4 Bent or worn splined shaft
5 Badly worn splines in driven plate hub
6 Distorted driven plate
7 Faulty engine or gearbox mountings

(e) Rattles

1 Check 4 and 5 in (d)
2 Weak diaphragm spring
3 Broken or loose spring in driven plate
4 Worn release mechanism
5 Excessive backlash in transmission
6 Wear in transmission bearings
7 Release bearing loose on mounting

(f) Tick or knock

1 Check 4 and 5 in (d)
2 Release bearing incorrectly installed
3 Loose flywheel

NOTES

CHAPTER 6

THE TRANSMISSION

6:1 Description

The transmission consists of a four-speed gearbox and differential unit. The casing is mounted in line with the engine and comprises clutch, gearbox and differential housings. Drive from the differential unit is transmitted to the rear wheels through two universally jointed drive shafts, removal and servicing of these shafts being described in **Chapter 7**. Gear selection is by means of a remote control linkage operated from the centrally mounted gearlever.

Note that certain special tools are necessary in order to carry out some of the overhaul procedures described in this chapter. If these factory tools or suitable substitutes are not available, the work should be carried out by a fully equipped service station.

6:2 Routine maintenance

Interim topping up procedures and periodic changing of the transmission oil should be carried out at the intervals specified in the manufacturer's service schedule. Transmission oil filler plug **A** and drain plug **B** are shown in **FIG 6:1**. When checking the oil level, clean away all dirt from around the filler and level plug before removing it. The oil level should be at the bottom of the threaded hole

when the car is standing on level ground. Add an approved grade of SAE 90 (not EP) transmission oil if necessary, then allow excess oil to drain away fully before refitting and tightening the plug. To change the oil, remove the drain plug and allow the old oil to drain into a suitable container. Refit and firmly tighten the drain plug, then fill the gearbox to the correct level as described previously.

6:3 Gearchange linkage

Adjustment:

Check gearchange linkage adjustment by selecting neutral then detaching the rubber boot from the base of the gearlever. In the neutral position, the gearlever should be centralised in the guide plate mounted on the car floor and should be vertical when viewed from the side. If not, raise and safely support the rear of the car then locate the gearchange linkage flexible coupling beneath the car, as shown in **FIG 6:2**.

Scribe a line across the coupling and clamp plate assembly (arrowed) so that the original position can be regained if necessary, then slacken the two bolts 3 to release flexible coupling 1 from gearchange rod 4. Move the flexible coupling within the limits allowed by the oversize mounting holes until the gearlever is in the centre

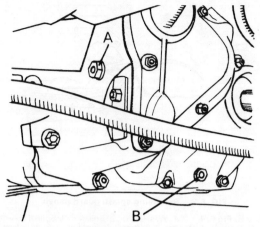

FIG 6:1   Transmission oil filler plug A and drain plug B

FIG 6:2   Gearchange linkage adjustment

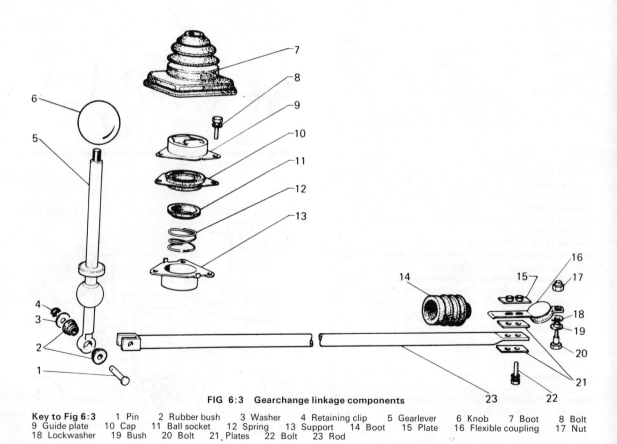

FIG 6:3   Gearchange linkage components

Key to Fig 6:3   1 Pin   2 Rubber bush   3 Washer   4 Retaining clip   5 Gearlever   6 Knob   7 Boot   8 Bolt
9 Guide plate   10 Cap   11 Ball socket   12 Spring   13 Support   14 Boot   15 Plate   16 Flexible coupling   17 Nut
18 Lockwasher   19 Bush   20 Bolt   21 Plates   22 Bolt   23 Rod

of the guide plate and vertical when viewed from the side. Firmly tighten the two bolts then recheck the adjustment. Refit the gearlever boot.

Gearchange linkage removal:

Refer to **FIG 6:3**. Remove rubber boot 7 from base of gearlever, then remove the three bolts 8 securing guide plate 9 to body panel. Lift the gearlever, guide plate and support assembly from the mounting, then remove retaining clip 4 and pin 1 to release gearlever, bushes and washer from gearchange rod. Remove bolt 20 securing flexible coupling to transmission selector shaft, then remove gear change rod rearwards to remove. Do not disturb bolts 22 securing flexible coupling to rod.

Refit the gearchange linkage in the reverse order of removal. On completion, check linkage adjustment as described previously and correct if necessary.

6:4 Transmission removal and refitting

Removal:

Refer to **Chapter 2** and remove the air cleaner and duct for carburetter cooling. Disconnect the battery. Refer to **Chapter 5** and remove clutch slave cylinder without disconnecting fluid hose.

Remove nuts and bolts holding transmission to engine crankcase which are accessible from above, then raise and safely support the rear of the car and remove the rear wheels. Fit suitable lifting equipment and tension sufficiently to take the weight of the engine.

Working from beneath the car, remove the three splash guard panels shown in **FIG 6:4**. Scribe or paint mark the gearchange linkage coupling and plates as shown in **FIG 6:2**, then remove both bolts 3 and collect the plates. Slacken bolt 2 and swing coupling 1 away from the work area.

Refer to **FIG 6:5**. Disconnect the connector 1 for reversing lights then remove the clamp holding wires to body. If seat belt interlock system is incorporated, disconnect the system wiring connector which is located inboard and forward of transmission near engine water hoses. Remove three bolts 2 securing starter motor, then move starter motor from transmission. Either disconnect wiring and remove starter motor completely, or support starter motor by tying to suitable adjacent component to prevent strain on wiring. Disconnect speedometer cable from transmission.

Refer to **FIG 6:6** and disconnect earth strap 1. Remove exhaust system 2 by detaching from exhaust manifold, removing two bolts and washers holding bracket to top of exhaust pipe then removing two bolts and washers securing pipe to crossmember 3. Refer to **Chapter 8** and remove the hub nuts securing drive shafts to wheel hubs. Remove two bolts and nuts securing suspension control arm to supports. Pull wheel hub from drive shafts then prevent shafts from coming out of transmission by suitably tying in place.

Remove the flywheel cover then remove the crossmember supporting engine. Remove remaining bolts and nuts securing transmission to engine. Using a suitable support and jack, or with the help of an assistant, support the weight of the gearbox while moving it away from the engine until the splined shaft is clear of the clutch. Lower the transmission assembly and remove from beneath the

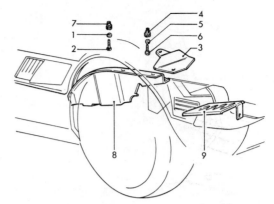

FIG 6:4   Removing splash guard panels

Key to Fig 6:4   1 Washer   2 Bolt   3 Splash guard   4 Fastener   5 Washer   6 Bolt   7 Fastener   8, 9 Splash guards

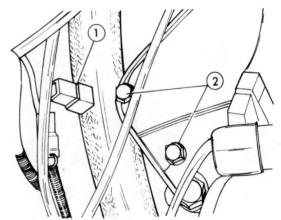

FIG 6:5   Reversing light connector 1 and starter mounting bolts 2

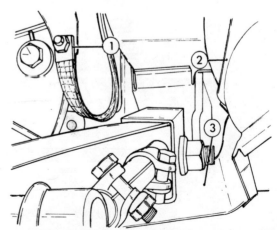

FIG 6:6   Earth strap 1, exhaust system 2 and crossmember 3

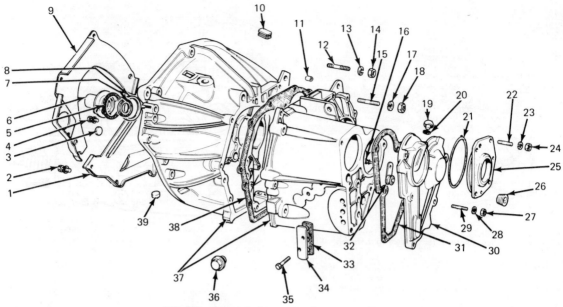

FIG 6:7 Transmission case and cover components

Key to Fig 6:7   1 Cover   2 Bolt and washer   3 Plug   4 Bolt and washer   5 Gasket   6 Cover   7 Seal   8 Plug   9 Cover
10 Plug   11 Dowel   12 Stud   13 Lockwasher   14 Nut   15 Stud   16 Bolt and washer   17 Lockwasher   18 Nut
19 Vent   20 Gasket   21 Seal   22 Stud   23 Lockwasher   24 Nut   25 Flange   26 Plug   27 Nut   28 Lockwasher
29 Stud   30 Cover   31 Gasket   32 Magnet   33 Gasket   34 Cover   35 Bolt   36 Plug   37 Castings   38 Gasket   39 Plug

car. **Do not allow the weight of the transmission to hang on the splined shaft while it is in the clutch unit, otherwise serious damage to clutch components may occur.**

Refitting:

This is a reversal of the removal procedure, observing the correct tightening torques for component fixings. Note that suspension components must be finally tightened with the car properly laden as described in **Chapter 8**. Take care to avoid clutch damage when entering splined shaft through clutch assembly. On completion, check

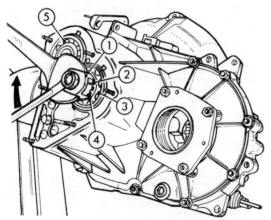

FIG 6:8 Compressing countershaft bearing spring washer

transmission oil level as described in **Section 6:2** and gearchange linkage adjustment as described in **Section 6:3**.

6:5 Transmission dismantling

Attach the transmission assembly to a suitable support stand, if available. If not, use suitable blocks of wood to hold the transmission in the required attitudes when dismantling.

Remove the drain plug and drain the transmission oil into a suitable container. Refer to **Chapter 8** and remove drive shafts from transmission. Remove release bearing and mechanism as described in **Chapter 5**. Refer to **FIG 6:7** and remove cover 30 with gasket 31. Use tool A.70284, or a tool made up from a suitable bolt, washer and piece of tube cut for circlip access, to compress the special spring washer as shown in **FIG 6:8**. Tighten the bolt so that tool 1 compresses the washer, then remove circlip 2 from countershaft 4. Remove circlip from main shaft bearing 5. Remove cover 34 shown in **FIG 6:7**, then remove the three detent springs and balls from the bores in the case. Remove bearings 3 and 5 from shafts (see **FIG 6:8**).

Refer to **FIG 6:7**. Remove the fixing nuts, then separate transmission case halves 37 and detach gasket 38. Refer to **FIG 6:9**. Remove screws retaining selector forks and dogs 1, 2, 3, 6 and 7, then remove rods, forks and dogs from their seats in housing. Remove nut 10 and detach selector lever support 9. Remove nut 4 and detach plate 3 retaining reverse shaft 11. Remove the reverse shaft. Remove main shaft assembly 12 and countershaft assembly 13 with gears, then remove differential assembly 14.

Refer to **FIG 6:10**. Remove screw retaining lever 1, then remove selector rod 2 as indicated by the arrow.

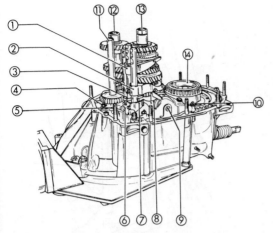

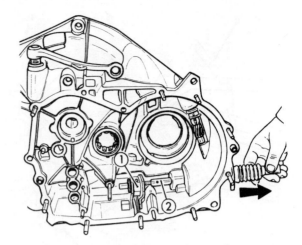

FIG 6:9   Removing selectors, gears and differential

FIG 6:10   Selector rod removal

Key to Fig 6:9   1 3rd and 4th gear selector fork   2 1st and 2nd gear selector fork   3 3rd and 4th gear dog   4 Nut   5 Plate   6 Reverse selector fork   7 1st and 2nd gear dog   8 Gear selector and engagement lever   9 Support   10 Nut   11 Reverse gearshaft   12 Mainshaft assembly   13 Countershaft assembly   14 Differential assembly

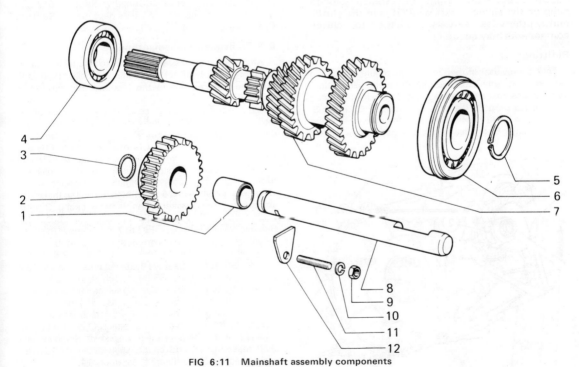

FIG 6:11   Mainshaft assembly components

Key to Fig 6:11   1 Bush   2 Gear   3 Seal   4 Bearing   5 Circlip   6 Bearing   7 Mainshaft   8 Shaft   9 Nut   10 Lockwasher   11 Stud   12 Plate

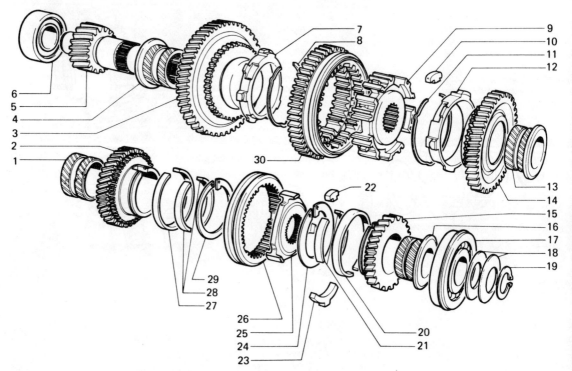

FIG 6:12   Countershaft assembly components

Key to Fig 6:12   1 Bush   2, 3 Driven gears   4 Bush   5 Countershaft   6 Bearing   7 Synchroniser   8 Spring   9 Hub
10 Pad   11 Spring   12 Synchroniser ring   13 Bush   14 Driven gear   15 Gear   16 Bush   17 Bearing   18 Spring washer
19 Circlip   20 Synchroniser ring   21 Spring   22, 23 Pads   24 Circlip   25 Hub   26 Sleeve   27 Synchroniser ring
28 Spring   29 Circlip   30 Sleeve

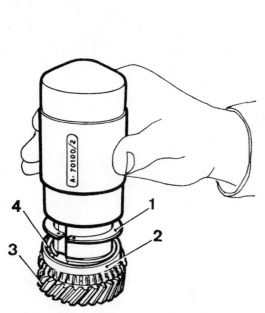

FIG 6:13   Reassembling synchroniser components

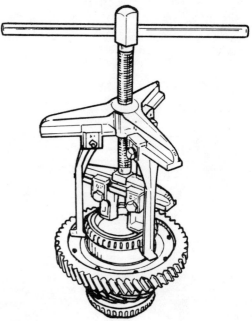

FIG 6:14   Removing bearing inner race from differential

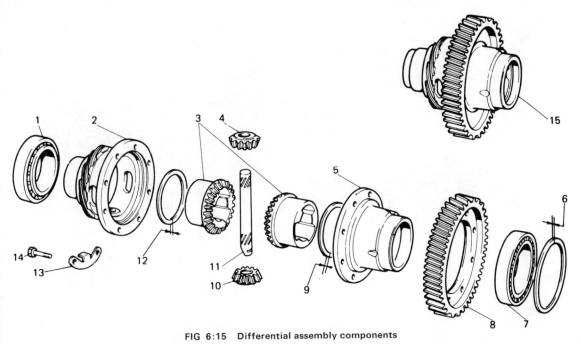

FIG 6:15 Differential assembly components

Key to Fig 6:15   1 Bearing   2 Half case   3 Side gears   4 Pinion gear   5 Half case   6 Ring   7 Bearing   8 Ring gear
9 Thrust washer   10 Pinion gear   11 Pinion shaft   12 Thrust ring   13 Lock plate   14 Bolt   15 Gear and case assembly

If necessary, dismantle mainshaft and countershaft gears into the order shown in **FIGS 6:11** and **6:12**.

Clean all parts thoroughly and examine the condition of the gears, synchromesh assemblies and selector mechanisms. Renew any part found worn or damaged. Check the synchroniser rings for wear and for a correct fit in their seats. There should be no noticeable play or looseness. Renew rings if necessary. Be sure that new rings are of the correct size. When seated in the synchromesh assembly, the outside diameter of first and second gear rings should be 76.31 ± 0.2mm (3.004 ± 0.008in) and third and fourth gear rings should be 66.22 ± 0.2mm (2.607 ± 0.008in) in diameter. Check the sliding sleeve hubs for nicks and damage to the sliding surfaces. If the splined parts of synchromesh assemblies do not slide smoothly, examine for burrs and remove any found with an oilstone. Serious damage to any part will dictate renewal. Reassembly of synchroniser components will be facilitated by the use of the special factory tool or other suitable tubular tool, as shown in **FIG 6:13**. Fit the synchroniser ring 2 to gear 3, then fit the spring 4 and circlip 1. Push the circlip into position using the special tool.

If the differential bearings are worn or damaged, remove the inner races from differential carrier using a suitable puller tool as shown in **FIG 6:14**. Use a suitable puller tool to remove the outer bearing races from the case. Collect the shims fitted between bearing outer race and the sealing cover. To dismantle the differential assembly, refer to **FIG 6:15**. Make a reference mark on half cases 2 and 5, so that they can be reassembled in their original relative positions. Remove the eight fixing bolts and separate the half cases, then remove lock plate from pinion shaft and drive the

shaft from the case. Remove the side gears, pinion gears and thrust washers. Clean all parts then examine them for wear or damage. Renew parts as necessary.

Reassemble the differential unit in the reverse order of dismantling. The assembled unit should be checked for backlash between side gears 3 and pinion gears 4 and 10 (see **FIG 6:15**). Backlash should not exceed 0.1mm (0.004in). Backlash exceeding the figures stated can be caused by excessive clearance requiring thrust washers of increased thickness, or by worn parts which must be renewed as necessary. If the original differential bearings and transmission case components are to be reassembled, the existing differential bearing packing shims should be refitted. If either differential bearings or transmission case have been renewed, the differential bearings must be correctly preloaded as described later.

When transmission overhaul is complete, reassemble the components in the reverse order of dismantling, using new gaskets throughout. Remove any burrs from mating faces of transmission case components. Lubricate all internal moving parts with the correct grade of transmission oil during reassembly. If necessary, carry out the following adjustments to ensure correct differential bearing preload.

Differential bearing setting:

Differential bearing preload must be correctly reset if either differential bearings or transmission case have been renewed. The work can be carried out without the need for special tools, in the following manner:

Refer to **FIG 6:16**. Place the outer ring of the carrier bearing in its seat and place the shims originally removed on top of the bearing. Place the retaining flange on shims,

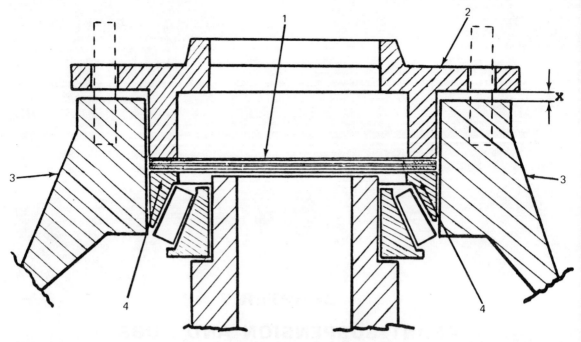

FIG 6:16 Setting differential bearing preload

Key to Fig 6:16 1 Shims 2 Retaining flange 3 Transmission housing 4 Bearing

then use feeler gauges to measure clearance **X** between flange and transmission housing. This should be 0.08 to 0.12mm (0.003 to 0.005in). If not, add or remove shims as necessary to bring within the limits stated. Install two nuts on studs which secure the flange, then tighten nuts alternately and evenly. Turn the differential unit through one full turn to set the bearings, then loosen nuts and recheck clearance. Modify shim thickness again if necessary. On completion, finally install the flange and tighten nuts to 2.5kgm (18lb ft).

6:7 Fault diagnosis

(a) Jumping out of gear

1 Excessively worn selector shafts
2 Worn synchromesh assemblies
3 Loose or worn selector fork or dog

(b) Noisy transmission

1 Insufficient oil
2 Bearings worn or damaged
3 Worn drive shaft joints
4 Worn gears or shafts
5 Worn synchromesh units

(c) Difficulty in engaging gear

1 Incorrect clutch adjustment
2 Faulty clutch components
3 Worn synchromesh assemblies
4 Worn selector shafts or forks
5 Gearchange linkage adjustment incorrect

(d) Oil leaks

1 Damaged joint gaskets
2 Worn or damaged oil seals
3 Faulty joint faces on transmission casings

CHAPTER 7

FRONT SUSPENSION AND HUBS

7:1 Description
7:2 Control arms and reaction struts
7:3 Wheel hubs and carriers

7:4 Suspension struts
7:5 Suspension geometry
7:6 Fault diagnosis

7:1 Description

Independent front suspension is by means of McPherson struts. These suspension struts incorporate telescopic hydraulic dampers and coil springs mounted between pressed steel cups. The damper units also act as pivots for the front wheel hub carriers, to accommodate steering movement. A section through a front suspension and hub assembly is shown in **FIG 7:1**, the inset showing details of suspension strut upper mounting.

The front wheel hub carrier assembly is located at the upper point by the damper unit attachment and at the lower point by a control arm and reaction strut. To accommodate suspension movement, control arm to carrier attachment is by means of a ball joint. The front wheel hubs are supported in wide twin-row ballbearings. All joints and pivots in the front suspension are lubricated for life, so apart from an occasional check on condition and security of components, no routine maintenance is required.

7:2 Control arms and reaction struts

Reaction struts mounting bushes and control arm inner mounting bush assembly can be renewed separately if worn or damaged, but if the ball joint is worn or damaged

the control arm must be renewed complete. Always renew the control arm assembly if the ball joint rubber boot is damaged, as the ingress of road dirt will cause rapid wear of the joint.

Reaction strut removal:

Refer to **FIG 7:2**. Remove self-locking nut 1 and washer 2, then remove bolts 12 and 13 securing reaction strut to control arm. Remove the strut, collecting and carefully noting the position of any shims fitted at the mounting bracket end.

Examine all parts for wear or damage and renew as necessary. Slight distortion of the reaction strut can be rectified at a service station, but major distortion will dictate renewal. Refit in the reverse order of removal, making sure that any shims are refitted in their original positions. Renew all self-locking nuts. On completion, it is recommended that suspension geometry be checked as described in **Section 7:5**.

Control arm removal:

Raise and safely support the front of the car, and remove the road wheel. Detach the reaction strut from control arm as described previously. **FIG 7:3** shows control arm

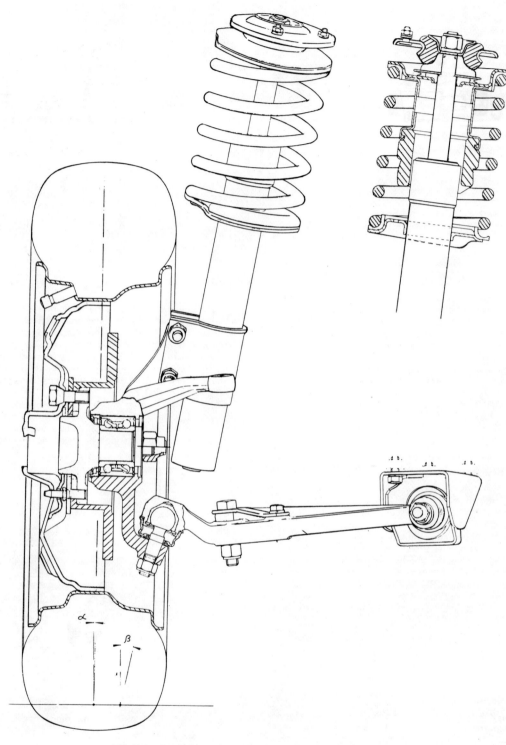

FIG 7:1 Section through front suspension and hub assembly

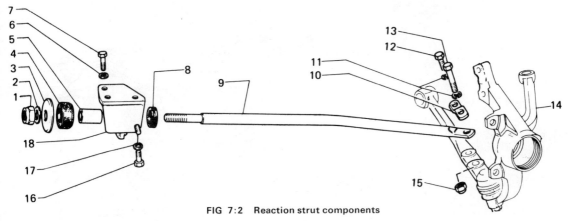

FIG 7:2 Reaction strut components

Key to Fig 7:2   1 Nut   2 Washer   3 Cup washer   4 Rubber bush   5 Spacer   6 Lock washer   7 Bolt   8 Rubber bush
9 Reaction strut   10 Lock plate   11 Lock washer   12, 13 Bolts   14 Hub carrier   15 Nut   16 Bolt   17 Washer
18 Mounting bracket

components. Remove nut 10, then use a suitable puller tool to disconnect ball joint from hub carrier 11. Remove nut 1 and bolt 9 to detach control arm.

Examine all components for wear or damage. If the ball joint or the control arm is faulty, the assembly must be renewed complete, but if the inner bushing is worn or damaged this can be renewed. However, as special tools and press equipment are needed to install the bushes And flare the ends of the inner spacer, the work should be carried out by a fully equipped service station.

Refit the components in the reverse order of removal, using new self-locking nuts. On completion, it is recommended that suspension geometry be checked as described **Section 7:5**.

7:3 Wheel hubs and carriers

Hub carrier removal:

Raise and safely support the front of the car, then remove the road wheel. If the hub assembly is to be dismantled after removal, have an assistant depress the brake pedal to lock the hub and disc against rotation, then slacken the hub retaining nut located on the inboard side. Remove brake caliper 5 and mounting 6 (see **FIG 7:4**) then support caliper so that hose is not strained, referring to **Chapter 10** for detailed instructions concerning brake system components. Remove bolt 1 and centring stud 2 securing disc 3 and plate 4.

Refer to **FIG 7:5** and remove nut 1 securing tie rod ball joint 2 to hub carrier 3. Use a suitable puller to disconnect ball joint from carrier. Remove nut 4 and disconnect control arm ball joint in a similar manner. Remove two nuts and bolts 6 securing hub carrier to suspension strut, then remove the carrier.

Hub bearing renewal:

Refer to **FIG 7:6**. Remove and discard the hub securing nut. Clamp hub carrier 3 in a vice having padded jaws, then use tool 8015 or other suitable drift 1 to drive hub 2 from carrier. Use tool A.57123 or similar to remove ring nut

securing bearing in carrier. Discard the nut as a new one must be used when reassembling. Refer to **FIG 7:7** and use tool 8015 or other suitable tool (1) to pull bearing 2 from carrier 3.

Make sure that the bore in the hub carrier is clean, then install a new hub bearing using tool 8015 or similar, as shown at 1 in **FIG 7:8**, to pull new bearing 2 into carrier 3. Refer to **FIG 7:9** and screw a new ring nut 2 into place. Use tool A.57123 or similar, in conjunction with a torque wrench, to tighten the ring nut to 6.0kgm (43.4lb ft). Use a suitable punch to stake the ring nut in position as shown by the arrow in **FIG 7:10**.

Refit the hub bearing in carrier, preferably using press equipment. Install the two washers and a new nut, then tighten nut to 14kgm (101lb ft). Stake the nut against rotation. If the hub cannot be held securely against

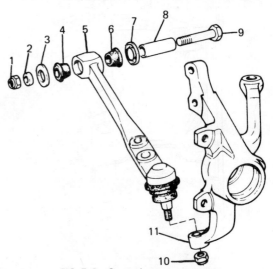

FIG 7:3 Control arm components

Key to Fig 7:3   1 Nut   2, 3 Washers   4 Rubber bush
5 Control arm   6 Rubber bush   7 Washer   8 Spacer
9 Bolt   10 Nut   11 Hub carrier

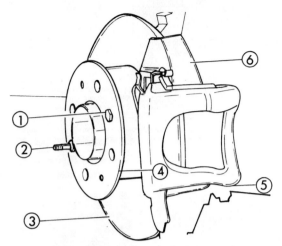

FIG 7:4   Brake caliper and disc mountings

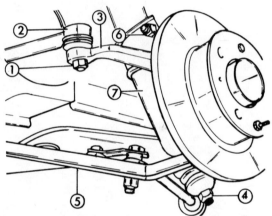

FIG 7:5   Hub carrier removal

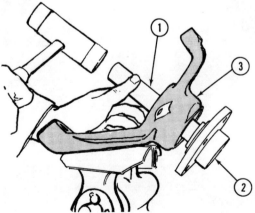

FIG 7:6   Removing hub from carrier

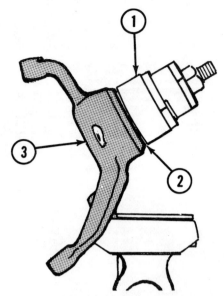

FIG 7:7   Hub bearing removal

rotation, screw the nut on as tightly as possible, then fully tighten to the correct torque after refitting the assembly, with the brake applied to lock the hub and disc assembly.

Refitting:

This is a reversal of the removal procedure. Reconnect all fixings shown in **FIG 7:5**, but do not fully tighten at this stage. Refit caliper and disc, fully tightening the attachments. Refit the road wheel and lower the car, then finally tighten the remaining fixings to recommended torque with the car in a laden condition. For these purposes, this is with two persons plus 20kg (44lb) of luggage, with tyres correctly inflated. On completion, it is recommended that suspension geometry be checked as described in **Section 7:5**.

7:4 Suspension struts

Removal:

Raise and safely support the front of the car, then remove the road wheel. Use a suitable jack or stand placed beneath the hub carrier to support the weight of the assembly. Refer to **FIG 7:11** and detach suspension strut 1 from upper mounting by removing the three nuts and washers 2. Remove the two nuts and bolts shown at 6 in **FIG 7:5**, then remove suspension strut from car.

Dismantling:

In order to remove coil springs from suspension strut it is essential to use a spring compressor tool, such as A.74241 or similar, as shown in **FIG 7:12**. If the factory tool is used, make sure that screws 1 are touching seat 2 for spring 3, and note that one screw at each end must be in the recess in the seat.

Refer to **FIG 7:13**. Make sure that screws 1 are properly located, then tighten the tool to compress the spring until it is clear of seat 2. Use a suitable spanner to slacken the damper retaining nut, using tool A.57020 or other suitable

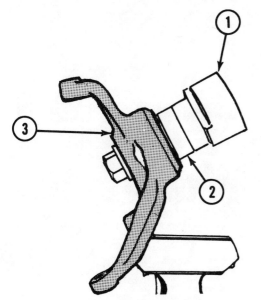

FIG 7:8   Hub bearing installation

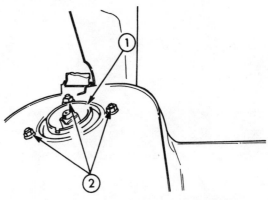

FIG 7:11   Suspension strut upper mounting

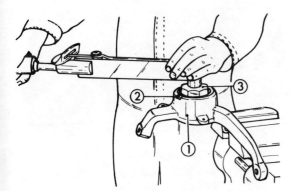

FIG 7:9   Tightening ring nut

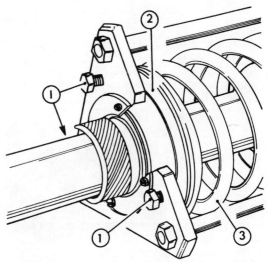

FIG 7:12   Installation of compressor tool A.74241

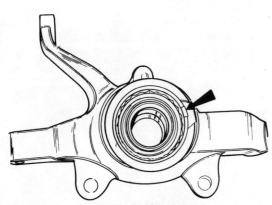

FIG 7:10   Staking ring nut

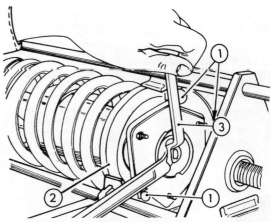

FIG 7:13   Slackening damper retaining nut

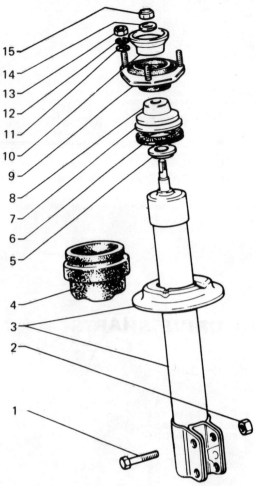

FIG 7:14 Damper mounting components

Key to Fig 7:14 1 Bolt 2 Nut 3 Damper and spring seat 4 Rubber pad 5 Thrust plate 6 Rubber ring 7 Washer 8 Spacer 9 Pad 10 Cup 11 Washer 12 Lock washer 13 Nut 14 Washer 15 Nut

tool (3) to hold the damper stud against rotation. Remove the nut, then detach the damper from coil spring. If the spring is not to be renewed, leave it compressed ready for installation.

If a damper unit is faulty it can be overhauled, but as this work requires the use of special tools and equipment it should be carried out by a fully equipped service station.

Refit the coil spring to damper in the reverse order of removal, making sure that the mounting components are correctly located as shown in **FIG 7:14**. When nut 15 has been fully tightened, remove the spring compressor.

Refitting:

This is a reversal of the removal procedure, renewing self-locking nuts and tightening all fixings to the recommended torque figures.

7:5 Suspension geometry

Due to the need for special optical measuring equipment for accurate results, the checking and adjusting of front wheel caster and camber angles should be carried out by a fully equipped service station. Checks must be carried out with the tyres inflated correctly and with the car unladen.

The correct caster and camber angles are given in **Technical Data**. Caster is adjusted by adding or removing shims between reaction struts and their front mounting brackets. Camber angles cannot be adjusted so if found to be incorrect all front suspension components should be examined for damage or distortion and parts renewed as necessary.

The method for setting the correct toe-in of front wheels is described in **Chapter 9**.

7:6 Fault diagnosis

(a) Wheel wobble

1 Worn hub bearings
2 Broken or weak front spring
3 Uneven tyre wear
4 Worn suspension linkage
5 Loose wheel fixings
6 Incorrect front wheel alignment

(b) Car pulls to one side

1 Unequal tyre pressures
2 Incorrect suspension geometry
3 Defective suspension bushes or damaged parts
4 Weak spring on one side
5 Fault in steering system

(c) Bottoming of suspension

1 Broken or weak coil spring
2 Defective damper

(d) Excessive body roll

1 Defective spring or damper

(e) Rattles

1 Check 2 and 4 in (a) and check (c)
2 Defective suspension strut mountings
3 Defective suspension arm bushes

(f) Suspension hard

1 Tyre pressures too high
2 Suspension arm ball joints stiff
3 Dampers faulty

CHAPTER 8

REAR SUSPENSION AND DRIVE SHAFTS

8:1 Description
8:2 Control arms and reaction struts
8:3 Wheel hubs and carriers
8:4 Suspension struts

8:5 Drive shafts
8:6 Suspension geometry
8:7 Fault diagnosis

8:1 Description

Independent rear suspension is by means of McPherson struts. The suspension struts consist of telescopic hydraulic dampers with coil springs mounted between two pressed steel support cups. Each rear wheel hub carrier is located at the upper point by the damper unit attachment and at the lower point by a control arm and reaction strut. The control arm inner mountings have provision for shim adjustment to set rear wheel geometry correctly. **FIG 8:1** shows a section through the rear suspension and hub assembly, control arm front (1) and rear (2) adjustment shim locations being shown inset. Ball joints are used at the control arm to hub carrier attachments in order to accommodate suspension movement.

The wheel hubs are carried on wide twin-row ballbearings. Each drive shaft is equipped with two constant-velocity joints, shaft ends being splined into wheel hubs and transmission differential gears.

All joints and pivots for rear suspension and drive shafts are sealed assemblies, so no routine maintenance is required between overhauls. However, an occasional check should be made on the condition of components and security of fixings, carefully examining the rubber

sealing boots on control arm ball joints and drive shaft constant-velocity joints. A damaged boot must be renewed without delay, otherwise rapid wear will result from the ingress of dirt.

8:2 Control arms and reaction struts

Control arm inner mounting bushes can be renewed after control arm removal and the rubber boot for outer ball joint can be renewed after disconnecting ball joint from hub carrier, but if the ball joint is worn or damaged the control arm must be renewed complete.

For some operations, it will be necessary first to detach the exhaust system after removing nuts securing pipe flange to manifold and bolts securing silencer to mounting bracket.

Control arm removal:

Raise and safely support the rear of the car, then remove the road wheel. **FIG 8:2** shows control arm components. Remove nut 11, then use a suitable puller tool to disconnect control arm ball joint from hub carrier 10. Remove the inner mounting nuts and washers, then remove the bolts and detach control arm from mountings. Carefully note positions of shims fitted at mounting points

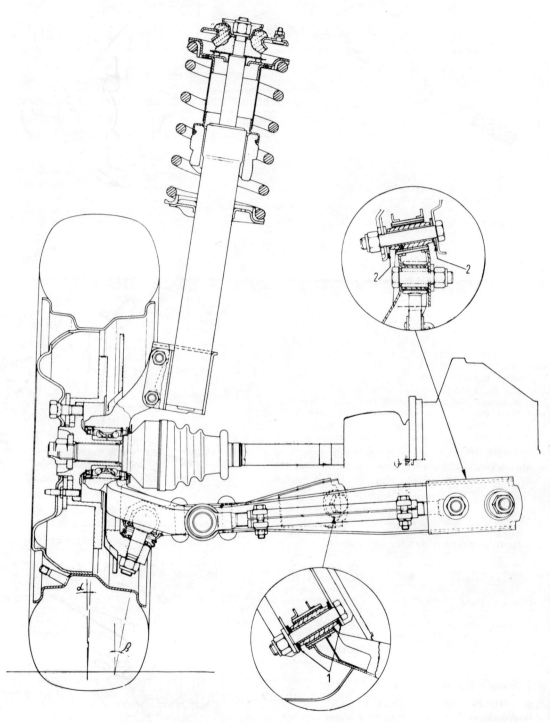

FIG 8:1   Section through rear suspension and hub assembly

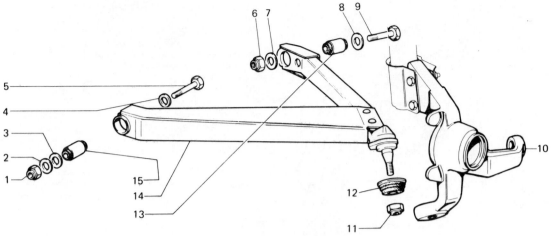

FIG 8:2   Control arm components

Key to Fig 8:2   1 Nut   2, 3, 4 Washers   5 Bolt   6 Nut   7, 8 Washers   9 Bolt   10 Hub carrier   11 Nut   12 Boot
13 Bush   14 Control arm   15 Bush

so that they can be refitted in their original positions. This is important to retain correct suspension geometry.

Check all parts for wear or damage and renew as necessary.

Refitting:

This is a reversal of the removal procedure, making sure that shims removed previously are refitted in their original positions. Use new self-locking nuts for control arm inner mountings, but do not fully tighten yet. When the road wheel has been refitted and the car lowered to the ground, load the car with two persons plus 20kg (44lb) of luggage and check that tyres are correctly inflated, then fully tighten control arm inner mountings to the recommended torque. On completion, it is recommended that suspension geometry be checked as described in **Section 8:6**.

Reaction strut removal:

Raise and safely support the rear of the car, then remove the road wheel. Disconnect the reaction strut ball joint from the hub carrier, then remove the control arm rear attachment bolt as described previously, noting the positions of shims. Do not slacken clamps for the reaction strut sleeve, unless parts are to be renewed.

Refitting:

This is a reversal of the removal procedure, making sure that adjustment shims are refitted in their original positions. Use new self-locking nuts, left loose until the car is properly laden as described previously, when final tightening to the recommended torque must be carried out. On completion it is recommended that suspension geometry be checked as described in **Section 8:6**, this being essential if the sleeve clamps have been loosened.

8:3   Wheel hubs and carriers

Hub carrier removal:

With the brakes applied by an assistant, slacken the hub nut. Raise and safely support the rear of the car, then

FIG 8:3   Removing brake components

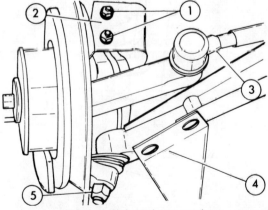

FIG 8:4   Hub carrier removal

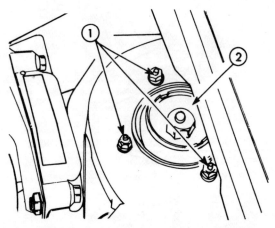

FIG 8:5 Suspension strut upper mounting

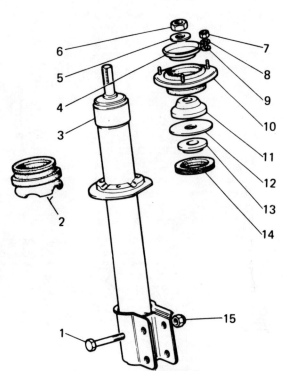

FIG 8:6 Damper mounting components

Key to Fig 8:6   1 Bolt   2 Rubber pad   3 Damper   4 Cup
5 Washer   6, 7 Nuts   8 Lock washer   9 Washer
10 Pad   11 Spacer   12 Washer   13 Thrust plate
14 Rubber ring   15 Nut

remove the road wheel and the hub nut. Refer to **FIG 8:3**. Remove brake caliper 1 and mounting bracket without disconnecting fluid hose, as described in **chapter 10**. Support caliper with length of wire so that hose is not strained. Remove bolts securing plate 2 and disc 3 to hub, then remove plate and disc.

Refer to **FIG 8:4**. Remove the two nuts and bolts 1 securing hub carrier to suspension strut. Remove nut 5 securing ball joint for control arm 4 and the nut securing ball joint for reaction strut 3, then separate ball joints from hub carrier using a suitable puller tool. Remove the hub carrier, supporting the drive shaft by wiring to suspension strut to avoid strain on the shaft joints.

Hub bearing renewal:

This work is carried out in the same manner as that described for front wheel bearings in **Chapter 7, Section 7:3**.

Refitting:

This is a reversal of the removal procedure, renewing all self-locking nuts. Tighten component fixings to the recommended torques. When the hub carrier and brake caliper assembly have been refitted, fit a new hub nut to the drive shaft and, with an assistant applying the brake pedal firmly, tighten to 14kgm (101lb ft). Stake the nut to lock against rotation, using a suitable punch to drive lock collar into the groove provided.

8:4 Suspension struts
Removal:

Raise and safely support the rear of the car, then remove the road wheel. Place a suitable stand or jack beneath the hub carrier to support the weight of the assembly. Refer to **FIG 8:5** and remove the three nuts and washers 1 securing suspension strut 2 in upper mounting. Remove the two nuts and bolts 1 (see **FIG 8:4**) securing suspension strut to hub carrier, then remove the unit from the car.

Dismantling:

Dismantling and servicing of suspension strut assemblies is carried out in a similar manner to that described for front suspension units described in **Chapter 7, Section 7:4**. Refer to **FIG 8:6** for identification of damper unit components.

Refitting:

This is a reversal of the removal procedure, using new self-locking nuts. Tighten upper and lower fixings to the recommended torques.

8:5 Drive shafts
Drive shaft removal:

Raise the rear of the car and support safely on floor stands, then remove the road wheel. Refer to **Chapter 6** and drain sufficient oil from the transmission to avoid leakage when the drive shaft is removed.

Refer to **Section 8:3** and carry out the instructions for removal of hub carrier, but do not disconnect carrier from suspension strut. Refer to **FIG 8:7** and remove the three bolts and washers 1 holding rubber boot 2 to differential flange. Pull the drive shaft 3 from transmission, then pull from hub and remove from beneath the car.

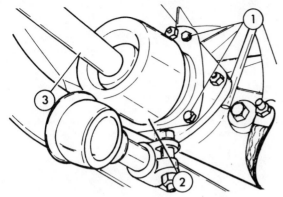

FIG 8:7   Driver shaft inner mounting

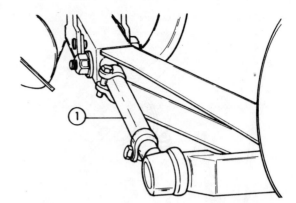

FIG 8:9   The wheel alignment adjusting sleeve

Dismantling:

Refer to **FIG 8:8**. Remove clamp 12, then pull back boot 6. Remove circlip 7 then pull constant-velocity joint 8 from drive shaft. If the boot is to be renewed, remove clamp 9 and detach the boot from shaft. Note that, when an outer boot is installed, it must be in contact with the shoulder on the drive shaft as shown by the arrow. Remove the inner boot if it is to be renewed.

Clean all grease from the constant-velocity joint using a suitable solvent. Examine all components for wear or damage and renew as necessary. Reassemble drive shaft in the reverse order of dismantling, lubricating constant-velocity joint sockets and boot with approved grease, using no more than $3\frac{3}{8}$oz of grease. Install the rubber boot securely, using new clamps if the originals are not in good condition.

Refitting:

This is a reversal of the removal procedure. On completion, refill the transmission with oil to the correct level as described in **Chapter 6**. Tighten the hub nut as described in **Section 8:3**.

8:6 Suspension geometry

Due to the need for special optical measuring equipment for accurate results, the checking and adjusting of rear wheel camber angles and wheel alignment should be carried out at a fully equipped service station.

Camber angle is adjusted by adding or removing shims at the control arm inner mounting positions (see **FIG 8:1**). Camber angle, with the car unladen, should be −1° 10' to −2° 10'.

Wheel alignment, with the car unladen, should be +9.0 to +13mm (+0.36 to +0.51in). Adjusting is carried out by slackening the securing clamps then rotating the reaction strut sleeve shown at 1 in **FIG 8:9**. The clamps must be securely tightened on completion.

8:7 Fault diagnosis

(a) Wheel wobble

1 Worn hub bearings
2 Weak rear springs
3 Uneven tyre wear
4 Worn suspension bushes
5 Loose wheel fixings

(b) Car pulls to one side

1 Unequal tyre pressures
2 Incorrect suspension geometry
3 Defective suspension bushes or damaged parts
4 Weak spring on one side
5 Fault in steering system

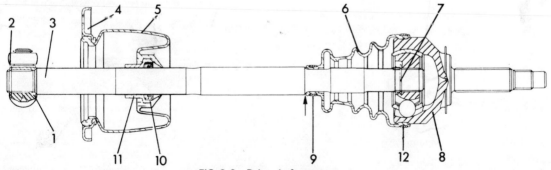

FIG 8:8   Drive shaft components

Key to Fig 8:8   1 Tripode joint   2 Circlip   3 Drive shaft   4 Flange   5 Inner sealing boot   6 Outer joint boot   7 Circlip
8 Constant-velocity joint   9 Clamp   10 Sealing ring   11 Bush   12 Clamp

(c) Bottoming of suspension

1 Broken or weak coil spring
2 Defective damper
3 Car overloaded

(d) Excessive body roll

1 Faulty spring or damper unit

(e) Rattles

1 Check 2 and 4 in (a)
2 Defective suspension strut or control arm bush

(f) Suspension hard

1 Tyre pressures too high
2 Control arm ball joints stiff
3 Dampers faulty

CHAPTER 9

THE STEERING GEAR

9:1 Description

Rack and pinion steering is employed. The pinion shaft is turned by the lower end of the steering column shaft and moves the rack to the left or right, transmitting the steering motion to the front wheels by means of the tie rods and the steering arms on hub carriers. The rack and pinion are held in mesh by a spring loaded adjustable yoke assembly. The steering gear housing is held to the car underbody by means of rubber bushed clamps. The steering column shaft is in two parts, the lower part being fitted with universal joints. The tie rod ends are connected to the steering arms by means of ball joint assemblies, the tie rods being threaded to the rack ends to allow for adjustment of front wheel alignment.

The steering gear and suspension ball joints are sealed assemblies, so no routine maintenance is necessary. However, the components should be regularly checked for wear or damage, paying particular attention to steering gear rubber gaiters and ball joint rubber dust covers. A damaged gaiter should be renewed without delay, otherwise rapid wear of the steering gear can occur due to the ingress of dirt. If a ball joint is worn or damaged, or if the rubber dust cover is damaged, the tie rod and ball joint unit should be renewed.

9:2 Steering wheel removal:

Disconnect the battery, then carefully remove horn button from centre of steering wheel. Remove the retaining nut, then pull the steering wheel from steering shaft. Refit in the reverse order of removal, making sure that the front wheels are in the straight ahead position and the steering wheel centralised. Tighten retaining nut to 5.0kgm (36.2lb ft).

9:3 Steering column:

Removal:

Disconnect the battery. Remove the five screws securing steering column covers, then remove the covers. Disconnect three electrical connectors and one wire. Remove steering wheel as described previously.

Refer to **FIG 9:1**. Remove two nuts and washers 1 and two bolts and washers 2 securing column assembly 3 to body panel. Refer to **FIG 9:2**. Remove bolt 1 and nut then slide turn indicator switch from shaft. Remove clamp bolt 4 securing universal joint on lower shaft 3 to upper shaft, then pull steering column shaft from joint. If lower shaft removal is necessary, remove the clamp bolt securing

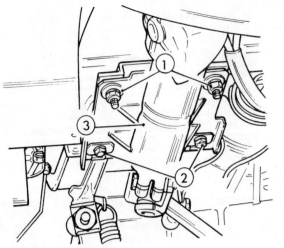

FIG 9:1   Steering column attachment points

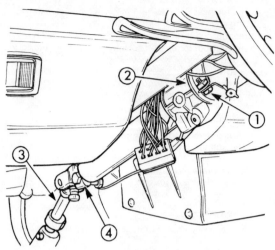

FIG 9:2   Indicator switch and upper universal joint

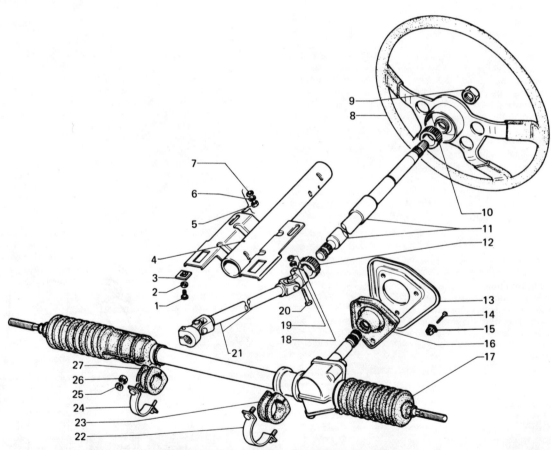

FIG 9:3   Column components and rack mounting details

Key to Fig 9:3   1 Bolt   2 Washer   3 Retainer   4 Support   5 Nut   6 Lockwasher   7 Washer   8 Steering wheel
9 Nut   10 Bushing   11 Steering column shaft   12 Bushing   13 Cover   14 Screw   15 Pad   16 Seal   17 Steering gear
18 Nut   19 Lockwasher   20 Bolt   21 Lower shaft   22 Clamp   23 Mounting rubber   24 Clamp   25 Lockwasher   26 Nut
27 Mounting rubber

lower universal joint to pinion shaft and remove lower steering shaft.

Steering column components are shown in **FIG 9:3**. Examine all components carefully and renew any found worn or damaged. Column bushes 10 and 12 should be removed if worn and new bushes pressed into place. If either universal joint is worn or damaged, renew the lower steering shaft 21 complete.

Refitting:

This is a reversal of the removal procedure. Make sure that the splines on upper column shaft and pinion shaft and in universal joint connections are clean, then reconnect joints and align bolt holes with grooves in shafts before installing and tightening clamp bolts and nuts.

9:4 Tie rods

Each tie rod and outer ball joint is manufactured as an assembly, which must be renewed complete if the ball joint is defective or the tie rod damaged.

Removal:

Raise and safely support the front of the car, then remove the road wheel. Refer to **FIG 9:4** and remove nut 1 securing ball joint to arm 3 on hub carrier. Use a suitable puller to separate ball joint from arm. Refer to **FIG 9:5**. Loosen locknut 1, while holding rack inner ball joint against rotation with a spanner on hexagon 2. Continue holding the inner ball joint against rotation while unscrewing tie rod and outer ball joint assembly, carefully counting the number of turns needed for removal.

Refitting:

Hold the rack ball joint against rotation and screw the tie rod into place by the same number of turns as counted during removal. Tighten the locknut to secure. Refit outer ball joint to steering arm, using a new self-locking nut. Refit the road wheel and lower the car, then check front wheel alignment as described in **Section 9:6**.

9:5 Steering gear
Removal:

Refer to **FIG 9:3**. From inside the car, remove clamp bolt from universal joints then remove cover 13 and seal 16. Disconnect tie rod outer ball joint from steering arm on each side, as described in **Section 9:4**. Remove the four bolts securing steering gear clamps to bodywork, then remove steering gear complete with tie rods.

Refitting:

Check mounting rubbers for steering gear clamps and renew if damaged or perished. Refit the steering gear in the reverse order of removal, using new self-locking nuts. On completion, check front wheel alignment as described in **Section 9:6**.

Overhaul:

Note that certain special tools will be necessary in order to carry out overhaul procedures. If these tools or suitable substitutes are not available, the work should be carried out by a fully equipped service station. Note that two

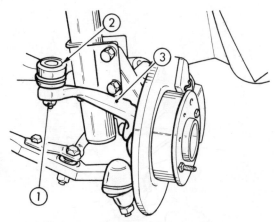

FIG 9:4 Disconnecting ball joint from hub carrier

alternative types of steering gear have been fitted in production, the earlier standard type and the later modified type (see **FIGS 9:6** and **9:7**). Instructions given in this section are for both types, unless otherwise stated.

Disconnect the tie rods from rack end ball joints as described in **Section 9:4**. Refer to **FIG 9:8** and loosen clamps 2. Drain the oil from the steering gear into a suitable waste container. Remove rubber gaiters 1 and the rubber insulators for steering gear mounting clamps. Remove the securing bolts, then detach plate 4 and remove gasket, spring, shims and yoke. Remove the fixing bolts and detach cover plate 3 then remove gasket, shims and pinion with bearing. Note that earth wire 5 attaches to bolt at cover 4.

Note that, on modified steering gear, rack ball joints have a threaded collar and if the joint is removed it must be renewed. For this reason, remove only one joint in order to remove the rack, leaving the other joint in place.

Carefully clamp the steering gear in a vice having padded jaws. On modified steering gear, release the

FIG 9:5 Tie rod inner connection

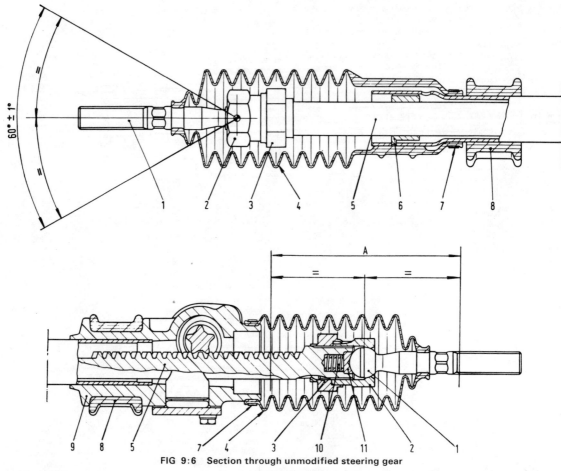

FIG 9:6 Section through unmodified steering gear

Key to Fig 9:6 1 Ball joint   2 Adjuster   3 Locknut   4 Rubber gaiter   5 Rod and rack   6 Bush   7 Clamp   8 Rubber pad
9 Steering gear housing   10 Spring   11 Ball pin cup   A=rack travel 117 ± 1.5mm $(4.606 \pm 0.059$in$)$

staking on the collar and ball joint then unscrew the ball joint. This must be discarded and a new joint used during reassembly. On unmodified steering gear, refer to **FIG 9:9** and release the staking on ring nuts 2. Unscrew the nuts, then slide off ball joints with sockets and springs.

Slide the rack from the steering gear, then remove the lower pinion bearing.

Servicing:

Thoroughly clean all parts and examine them for wear or damage. Check the rubber gaiters for splits, holes or perished conditions and check that their fixing clamps are in good order. Check the bearings for wear by pressing and turning them by hand. Check the bushes in the housing for wear or scored surfaces and ensure that the rack moves smoothly in the bushes without excessive play. If necessary, remove the old bushes and install new ones as shown in **FIG 9:10**. Use tool A.74347 or other suitable driver (1) to install bushes 2 until the tabs 3 on bushes engage in slots 4 provided in housing 5. Check the rack for

wear, damage or chipped teeth. Check the rack yoke for wear or scoring and the pinion for chipped teeth or other damage. Renew all worn or damaged parts. Always use new gaskets and seals during reassembly.

Reassembly and adjustment:

Support the steering gear horizontally in a vice having padded jaws, with the cover face upwards. Fit the pinion lower bearing in the housing, using tool A.74219 or other suitable driver. Engage the smooth end of the rack into the supporting bush, turning the rack as necessary to facilitate this operation. Turn the rack to bring the teeth towards the centre line of the pinion seat. Fit the pinion and upper bearing, engaging pinion with rack teeth. **FIG 9:11** shows a section through the assembly. The pinion must now be adjusted by selecting appropriate shims, in the following manner.

Refer to **FIG 9:12**. Using the special gauge **C**, apply sufficient load on the outer race of upper bearing to take up all end play, as shown by the arrow. Use feeler gauges to

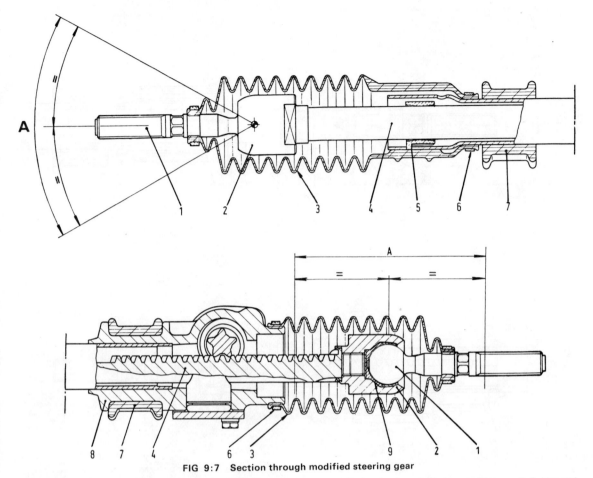

FIG 9:7 Section through modified steering gear

Key to Fig 9:7   1 Ball joint   2 Ball joint head   3 Rubber gaiter   4 Rod and rack   5 Bush   6 Clamp   7 Rubber pad
8 Steering gear housing   9 Ball joint socket   A = rack travel 117 ± 1.5mm (4.606 ± 0.059in)

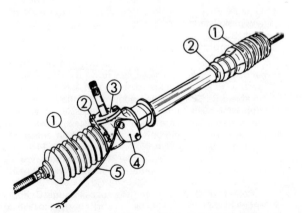

FIG 9:8 Steering gear gaiters and cover plates

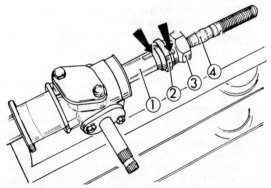

FIG 9:9 Rack ball joint removal. Arrows indicate staking points

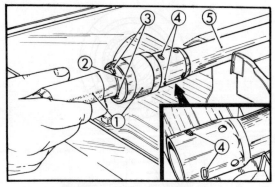

FIG 9:10   Rack bush installation

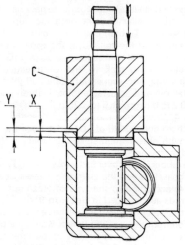

FIG 9:12   Adjusting pinion bearings

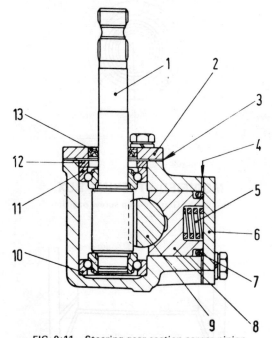

FIG 9:11   Steering gear section across pinion

Key to Fig 9:11   1 Pinion shaft   2 Cover plate   3 Gasket
4 Rack yoke shims   5 Spring   6 Yoke cover plate
7 Sealing ring   8 Rack yoke   9 Rack   10 Pinion lower
bearing   11 Pinion upper bearing   12 Pinion shims   13 Seal

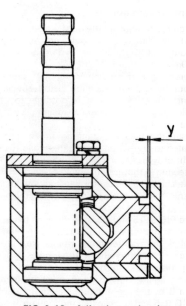

FIG 9:13   Adjusting rack yoke

measure dimension **X**. A suitable shim **S** must be selected
so that $S = Y - (X + 0.05 \text{ to } +0.13\text{mm})$. Note that shims are
available in 0.12, 0.20, 0.25 and 2.5mm thicknesses.

Coat the gasket and threads of retaining bolts with a
suitable sealing compound, then install gasket, plate,
washers and bolts. Tighten bolts alternately and evenly,
then install the pinion seal. Check that the pinion turns
freely without sticking, even without the yoke installed.
The rack must move smoothly and freely over its entire
travel. Move the rack to the centre position, then adjust the
yoke in the following manner.

Refer to **FIG 9:13**. Install rack yoke and cover plate as
shown, then turn pinion 180° in both directions to settle
the assembly and return the rack to the centre position. Use
feeler gauges to measure distance **Y** between steering gear
and cover plate. Suitable shims **S** must be selected so that
$S = Y + 0.05 \text{ to } +0.13\text{mm}$. Note that yoke shims are
available in 0.10 and 0.15mm thicknesses. Assemble the
spring and sealing ring on yoke, coat surfaces of shims
with suitable sealing compound, then install shims, cover
plate and fixing bolts. Check that rack still moves smoothly
over its entire travel.

On modified steering gear, lubricate new ball joint with oil then screw collar of joint onto rack up to end of threaded section. Tighten collar to 7.5kgm (54.25lb ft). Stake the inside of the collar over the edge of rack rod.

On unmodified steering gear, refer to **FIG 9:9** and screw nuts 2 onto rack to end of threaded section. Assemble spring and socket, lubricate ball joint with oil, then install pin and adjustable joint. Tighten joint until a force of 0.2 to 0.5kgm (1.5 to 3.25lb ft) is needed to move ball pins 4. Check that the pins can describe a rotation cone with an apex angle of 60° ±1°. Lock the heads in position with nuts 1, then stake the heads at the points indicated by the arrows.

Fit the rubber gaiters over ball joints and into position on steering gear. Position the clamping screws as shown in **FIG 9:14**, according to the type of steering gear fitted. Refit tie rods as described in **Section 9:4**.

Refit the steering gear as described previously. On completion, turn the steering fully towards the passenger side of the car, then raise and safely support the front of the car on the driver's side. Release the clamp for rubber gaiter on driver's side, then use a suitable syringe to inject 0.14 litre of SAE 90 EP oil into the rubber gaiter. On completion, refit the gaiter correctly and clamp in place, then lower the car. Carefully road test to check steering gear operation.

9:6 Front wheel alignment

When correctly adjusted the front wheels will converge slightly at the front when viewed vertically from above. The amount of convergence, known as toe-in, should be 2.0 to 4.0mm (0.079 to 0.157in).

Measurement and adjustment should preferably be carried out by a service station using special optical equipment, but failing this it is possible to obtain an acceptable degree of accuracy using the following procedure.

Make sure that the car is standing on level ground with tyres inflated to correct pressures, then load the car with the weight of two persons plus 20kg (44lb) of luggage. Set the steering in the straight ahead position. Release the handbrake and push the car forwards slightly to settle the components, then stop the car by applying the handbrake only.

Refer to **FIG 9:15** and measure distance between outer wheel rims at rear of wheel and level with wheel centre height. Mark the two reference points with chalk, then push the car slowly forwards to turn wheels through 180° and bring chalk marks to the front. Measure between the chalk marks again; dimension **A** must be greater than dimension **B** by the toe-in figure stated. If outside limits, refer to **FIG 9:5** and slacken locknut 1 on each side of the car. Use a spanner on hexagon 2 to rotate rack ball joints equally on each side until toe-in is correct, then firmly tighten locknuts and recheck.

9:7 Fault diagnosis

(a) Wheel wobble

1 Unbalanced wheels and tyres
2 Slack steering connections
3 Incorrect steering geometry
4 Excessive play in steering gear
5 Faulty suspension
6 Worn hub bearings

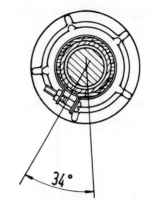

UNMODIFIED STEERING BOX

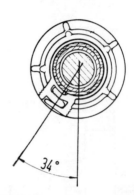

MODIFIED STEERING BOX

FIG 9:14   Gaiter clamp screw position

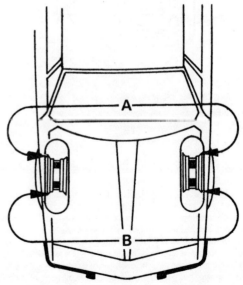

FIG 9:15   Checking front wheel toe-in

(b) Heavy steering

1 Incorrect steering geometry
2 Very low tyre pressures
3 Lack of lubricant
4 Wheel alignment incorrect
5 Rack adjustment too tight
6 Steering column shaft bent
7 Tight bearings

(c) Wander

1 Check 2, 3 and 4 in (a)
2 Uneven tyre pressures
3 Uneven tyre wear
4 Ineffective dampers

(d) Lost motion

1 Loose steering wheel
2 Worn rack and pinion teeth
3 Worn ball joints
4 Worn suspension strut swivels
5 Worn universal joints
6 Slack pinion bearings

CHAPTER 10

THE BRAKING SYSTEM

10:1 Description

Disc brake units are fitted at all four wheels, operated from the brake pedal through a dual circuit hydraulic system. The master cylinder, which draws fluid from twin reservoirs, is operated from the brake pedal by a short pushrod. Separate outlets from the master cylinder are coupled, via the brake pipes and hoses, to the disc brake caliper at each front wheel. A third outlet feeds the pipelines to the rear brake units. The front and rear brake circuits are operated simultaneously but independently from the two separate fluid chambers of the master cylinder. This dual circuit system is provided as a safety factor as, if one circuit should fail for any reason, the remaining circuit will provide effective braking power.

The handbrake operates on the rear disc brakes only, through a rod and cable linkage.

10:2 Routine maintenance

Regularly check the level of fluid in the master cylinder reservoirs and replenish if necessary. The reservoirs are located in the front luggage compartment. Wipe dirt from around each reservoir cap before removing it and check that the vent hole in the cap is unobstructed. If frequent topping up is required the system should be checked for leaks, but it should be noted that, with disc brake systems, the fluid level will drop gradually over a period of time, due to the movement of caliper pistons compensating for friction pad wear. The recommended brake fluid is Fiat Special Blue Label. **Never use anything but top quality universal disc brake fluid.**

Checking brake pad lining thickness:

The thickness of friction linings on front and rear brake pads should be checked at regular intervals. To do this, raise the front or rear of the car as appropriate and support safely on floor stands. Remove the road wheels. Look into the caliper and gauge remaining thickness of friction linings, which are adjacent to the brake disc. If the lining on any pad has worn to a thickness of 2.0mm (0.08in), or if any lining is cracked or oily, all four friction pads at front or rear, as appropriate, must be renewed. **Do not renew pads singly or on one side of the car only as uneven braking will result.** Instructions for renewing brake pads are given in **Section 10:3**.

Brake adjustment:

No adjustments are required for the service brakes. The disc brakes are self-adjusting, due to the action of the

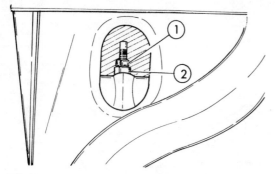

FIG 10:1 Handbrake cable locknut 1 and adjusting nut 2

operating pistons in the calipers. These pistons are returned to the rest position after each brake operation by the piston seals, the seals being slightly stretched during brake application. As the friction pads wear, the piston stroke is increased and the piston will travel further than before and move through the stretched seal a little, the seal returning the piston to a new position nearer the pads when the brakes are released. In this manner the piston stroke remains constant regardless of the thickness of friction pads.

Handbrake adjustment:

After servicing operations have been carried out on the handbrake mechanism components, or if the operating cables have stretched in service, the linkage should be adjusted. A need for adjustment is indicated if handbrake lever travel is excessive, but always check rear brake friction pads first and renew if necessary, as described previously.

Raise and safely support the rear of the car. Chock the front wheels against rotation then fully release the handbrake. From the fully off position, apply the handbrake lever by three or four clicks on the ratchet. Refer

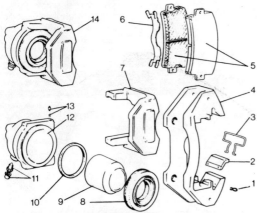

FIG 10:2 Front brake caliper components

Key to Fig 10:2 1 Retaining pin 2 Locking block 3 Spring
4 Mounting bracket   5 Brake pad   6 Pad retaining spring
7 Caliper yoke   8 Rubber boot   9 Piston   10 Seal
11 Bleed screw and dust cap   12 Cylinder   13 Spring and
dowel 14 Complete caliper assembly

to **FIG 10:1** and remove the cover from the access hole. Slacken locknut 1, then tighten adjusting nut 2 until resistance to turning by hand can be felt at the rear wheels. Now tighten the adjuster a little more until the rear wheels are just locked against rotation by hand. Release the handbrake and check that the rear wheels are completely free to turn, without any sign of binding. If necessary, slacken the adjusting nut a little. On completion, hold the adjusting nut with one spanner and firmly tighten the locknut against it with a second spanner.

10:3 Disc brakes

Front brake caliper components and rear brake caliper components are shown in **FIGS 10:2** and **10:3** respectively.

Brake pad renewal:

When working on front brake units, apply the handbrake, raise and safely support the front of the car, then remove the road wheel. For rear brake units, raise and safely support the rear of the car, chock the front wheels against rotation and fully release the handbrake, then remove the road wheel.

Refer to **FIG 10:4**. Remove retaining pins 1 from locking blocks 2, then carefully tap locking blocks from caliper 3. Refer to **FIG 10:5** and pull caliper 1 from mounting bracket 5, without disconnecting fluid hose 4. Take care to avoid strain on the hose. Collect brake pads 2, the shaped wire spring and the pad retaining spring. Support the caliper by wiring to the suspension so that the hose is not strained. **Do not touch the brake pedal when any caliper is removed.**

If the pads are being removed as part of other servicing operations only and are not to be renewed, mark them so that they will be refitted at the same side of the caliper from which they were removed and take care not to contaminate linings with dirt or grease.

Install the pads in the reverse order of removal, pushing the operating piston in the caliper to the bottom of its bore after pad installation by carefully pulling the pads apart. Take care not to contaminate friction lining material during this operation. Note that this operation will cause the fluid level in the reservoir to rise, so it may be necessary to syphon off a little of the fluid to prevent leakage. Note that brake fluid is poisonous and that it can damage paintwork. Make sure that the pad springs and locking blocks are correctly located and use new retaining pins if the originals are not in good condition. On completion, operate the brake pedal several times to move the brake pads close to the disc, otherwise the brakes may not operate correctly the first time that they are applied. Finally, check and if necessary correct fluid level in supply reservoir.

Caliper removal and refitting:

If the caliper is to be overhauled, remove it from the mounting bracket and detach brake pads as described previously, then disconnect brake hose from caliper and collect the sealing washers. Immediately plug the end of the hose as it is detached, to prevent leakage and ingress of dirt. On rear brake units, refer to **FIG 10:6** and, after removal of hose 1 as previously described, disconnect handbrake cable 3 from caliper 2. If necessary, remove caliper mounting bracket from hub carrier.

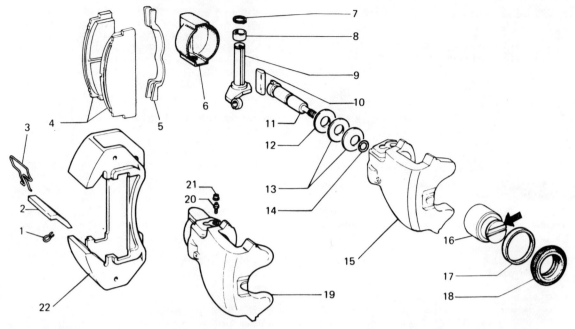

FIG 10:3   Rear brake caliper components

Key to Fig 10:3   1 Retaining pin   2 Locking block   3 spring   4 Brake pads   5 Pad retaining spring   6 Rubber boot
7 Locking ring   8 Spacer   9 Handbrake shaft   10 Pawl   11 Plunger   12, 13 Spring washers   14 Seal   15 Caliper
cylinder   16 Piston   17 Seal   18 Rubber boot   18 Complete caliper assembly   20 Bleed screw   21 Dust cover
22 Mounting bracket

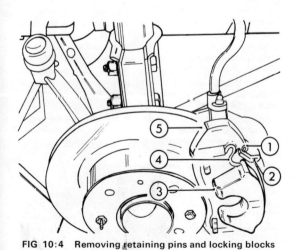

FIG 10:4   Removing retaining pins and locking blocks

Key to Fig 10:4   1 Retaining pin   2 Locking blocks   3 Caliper
4 Spring   5 Mounting bracket

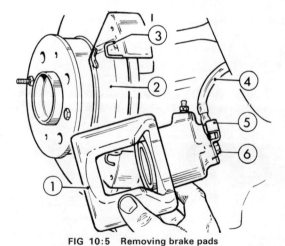

FIG 10:5   Removing brake pads

Key to Fig 10:5   1 Caliper   2 Brake pad   3 Spring
4 Brake hose   5 Mounting bracket   6 Bolt

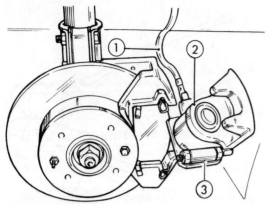

FIG 10:6   Disconnecting handbrake cable from caliper

Key to Fig 10:6 1 Brake hose 2 Caliper 3 Handbrake cable

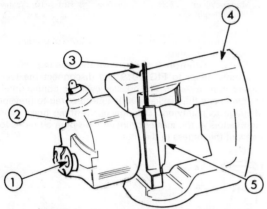

FIG 10:7   Removing caliper from yoke

Key to Fig 10:7 1 Hose connection 2 cylinder 3 Thin rod 4 Yoke 5 Rubber boot

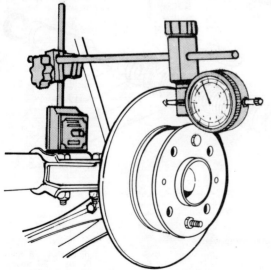

FIG 10:8   Checking brake disc for distortion

If the caliper assembly is to be removed to provide access for other servicing operations, raise and safely support the car then remove the road wheel. Remove the two mounting bolts securing caliper mounting bracket to hub carrier, then carefully detach the assembly and support by wiring to the underbody to prevent strain on the brake hose. Do not touch the brake pedal while the caliper is removed.

Refit the caliper in the reverse order of removal. If the caliper was removed complete without disconnecting the hose, carefully fit the unit into place making sure that the brake pads are positioned correctly at each side of the disc. If necessary, carefully pull the pads apart to provide extra clearance, taking care not to get dirt or oil onto the friction linings.

If the fluid hose was disconnected from the caliper, make sure that it is correctly reconnected with sealing washers in place and that the hose is not twisted or strained when the caliper is refitted. On completion, bleed the brakes as described in **Section 10:5**.

Caliper overhaul:

Remove the caliper from mounting bracket as described previously.

Front brake unit:

Brush road dirt and rust from the caliper then clean the outside of the assembly using methylated spirits. Refer to **FIG 10:7**. Remove the rubber boot 5, then depress the dowel using a thin rod 3 and separate cylinder 2 from yoke 4. Use compressed air at brake hose connection 1 to eject the piston from caliper. Do this carefully to avoid excessive pressure which would cause the piston to be ejected at high speed, as this may cause accidental damage or injury.

Refer to **FIG 10:2** and use a thin plastic or wooden rod to remove seal 10 from cylinder bore, taking care not to damage bore surfaces. Clean all internal parts with methylated spirits or the correct grade of brake fluid. **Do not use any other cleaning fluid or solvent.** Examine for signs of wear or scoring on the cylinder and piston surfaces. Renew all rubber seals and dust boots and any other part found defective during inspection. Dip the internal parts in clean brake fluid and assemble them wet. Observe absolute cleanliness to prevent the entry of dirt or any trace of oil or grease. Use the fingers only to fit the rubber piston seals to prevent damage. Reassemble the remaining caliper components in the reverse order of dismantling, then refit the caliper as described previously.

Rear brake unit:

Rear brake calipers are dismantled in a similar manner to that described previously for front brake units, but note that the piston is threaded onto the handbrake mechanism plunger shown at 11 in **FIG 10:3**. To remove the piston, use a suitable screwdriver to turn the piston anticlockwise until it is free of the threads, then use compressed air as described previously to eject the piston.

Service the components as previously described for front brake units, additionally checking components for handbrake mechanism, as shown in **FIG 10:3**. When reassembling, note that the piston must be screwed fully into place then aligned as shown in **FIG 10:3**, with the mark (arrowed) towards bleed screw (20) side of caliper. This done, push piston to bottom of its bore. On completion, refit the caliper as described previously then adjust handbrake mechanism as described in **Section 10:2**.

Brake discs:

To remove a brake disc, raise and safely support the car then remove the road wheel. Remove the brake caliper complete with mounting bracket as described previously, then remove the fixing screw and stud and detach plate and brake disc.

Check the surface of the disc for excessive wear or damage. Light score marks are unimportant, but deep scoring will dictate resurfacing of the disc at a service station or renewal if this remedial treatment would require the removal of too much metal. Note that minimal allowable thickness of disc after resurfacing is 9.35mm (0.368in).

Brake discs should be checked for distortion while properly installed on the hub, using a dial gauge assembly as shown in **FIG 10:8**. Rotate the disc through one full turn and check maximum indicator reading, which should not exceed 0.15mm (0.06in). If distortion is excessive, it may be possible to resurface the disc as described previously, but excessive distortion which cannot be cured by this method will dictate renewal of the disc.

10:4 The master cylinder

Removal:

Use a suitable syringe to drain the contents of brake fluid reservoir, keeping the fluid perfectly clean if it is to be re-used, but noting that it is recommended that all used

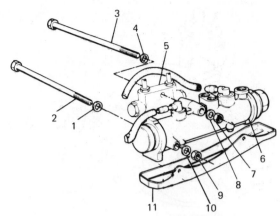

FIG 10:9 Master cylinder removal

Key to Fig 10:9 1 Washer 2, 3 Bolts 4 Washer 5 Switch 6 Master cylinder 7 Nut 8 Washer 9 Nut 10 Washer 11 Mounting bracket

fluid be discarded and new fluid of the correct grade used for topping up later.

Refer to **Chapter 9** and remove the steering column assembly. Refer to **FIG 10:9** and disconnect the feed hoses from reservoir and master cylinder connections, catching any fluid spillage with a piece of rag to prevent damage to paintwork. Disconnect the three brake pipe connectors at the master cylinder, then plug all pipes to prevent the ingress of dirt.

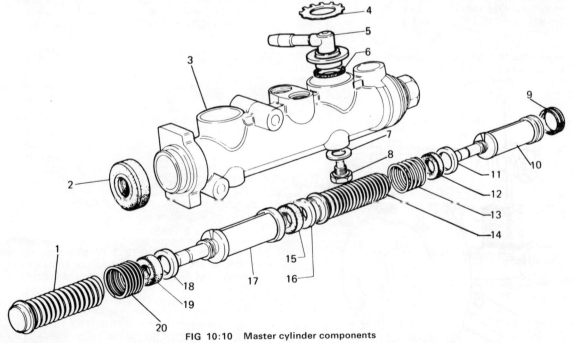

FIG 10:10 Master cylinder components

Key to Fig 10:10 1 Spring 2 Boot 3 Master cylinder 4 Lockplate 5 Connector 6 Seal 7 Sealing washer 8 Stop screw 9 Seal 10 Piston 11 Spacer 12 Seal 13, 14 Springs 15 Seal 16 Spacer 17 Piston 18 Spacer 19 Seal 20 Spring

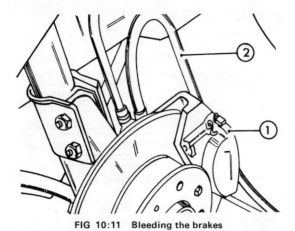

FIG 10:11 Bleeding the brakes

Remove bolts 2 and 3 securing master cylinder to support bracket 11, then carefully pull master cylinder away from operating pushrod and remove from the car.

Servicing:

Refer to **FIG 10:10**. Remove the boot 2, then remove the primary piston, springs, washers and seals, then partially release the stop screw 8 and remove the secondary piston assembly. Note that secondary piston assembly components must be retained in the bore by the stop screw when the master cylinder is reassembled. If necessary, remove connector 5 with lockplate 4 and seal 6. Discard all rubber parts and thoroughly clean the remaining parts in methylated spirits or the correct grade of brake fluid only. Inspect all parts for scoring, wear or damage. Make sure that the compensating ports in the

body are clear. Check the pistons and cylinder bores for rust marks and scoring, which would dictate renewal of the affected component. Always renew any part if its serviceability is in doubt. Cylinder bores should have a mirror finish, but if not perfectly smooth it is possible for the bore to be honed at a service station, but note that bore diameter must not be increased.

Coat all parts with clean brake fluid and assemble them wet. Reassemble the secondary piston assembly and insert it into the cylinder bore, pressing down the bore with a suitable tool while the stop screw is tightened, taking care not to damage the bore. Refit the primary piston and all other components in the reverse order of dismantling. Use the fingers only to fit the new rubber parts to prevent damage and observe absolute cleanliness to avoid the entry of dirt or grease.

Refitting:

This is a reversal of the removal procedure, making sure that all pipes and hoses are properly reconnected in their correct positions. On completion, top up the fluid in the supply reservoir to the correct level, then bleed the brakes as described in the next section.

10:5 Bleeding the system

This is not routine maintenance and it is only necessary if air has entered the system due to parts being dismantled, or because the fluid level in the supply reservoir has been allowed to drop too low. The need for bleeding is indicated by a spongy feeling at the brake pedal accompanied by poor braking performance. This must not be confused with the sharp drop in brake efficiency accompanied by greater pedal travel which indicates that one of the dual braking circuits has failed. This latter condition must be investigated immediately and the fault rectified.

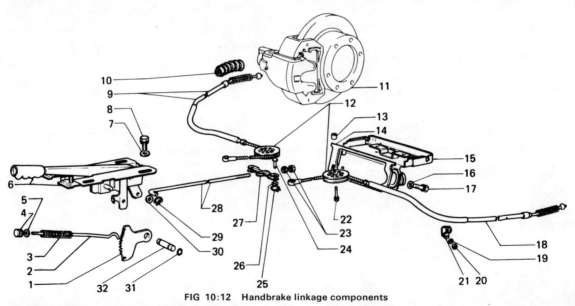

FIG 10:12 Handbrake linkage components

Key to Fig 10:12   1 Ratchet   2 Rod   3 Spring   4 Button   5 Rubber ring   6 Lever assembly   7 Washer   8 Bolt   9 cable   10 Boot   11 Disc   12 Pulleys   13 Spacer   14 Gasket   15 Support bracket   16 Washer   17 Bolt   18 Cable   19 Lockwasher   20 Nut   21 Clamp   22 Bolt   23 Nuts   24 Pin   25 Clip   26 Washer   27 Equaliser   28 Operating rod   29 Clip   30 Washer   31 Lock ring   32 Pin

If work has been carried out on the front brakes only or the rear brakes only, then it will normally only be necessary to bleed the circuit (front or rear) that is affected, as the other system should not have been disturbed. If both circuits have been disturbed, or if braking performance is poor, bleeding should be carried out at all four wheels. Bleeding must be carried out in the following sequence: rear wheel furthest from master cylinder, opposite rear wheel, front wheel furthest from master cylinder, opposite front wheel. **Do not bleed the brakes with any caliper removed or with any brake line disconnected.**

Check the fluid level in supply reservoir and top up if necessary. Clean the bleed screw dust caps and the area around the bleed screw to remove all dirt and rust. Remove the cap from bleed screw on the appropriate caliper 1 and attach a length of rubber tube 2 to the screw as shown in **FIG 10:11**. Lead the free end of the tube into a transparent container and add sufficient brake fluid to safely cover the end of the tube. Loosen the bleed screw and have an assistant press the brake pedal quickly to the floor and allow it to return slowly. Wait a few seconds for the master cylinder to refill with fluid then repeat the operation. Continue until no air bubbles can be seen in the fluid flowing from the tube into the container. Check and top up fluid level in the reservoir at frequent intervals during the operation, as if the level falls too low air will be drawn into the system and the operation will have to be restarted. When the fluid is free from air bubbles, hold the pedal to the floor at the end of a downstroke and tighten the bleed screw. Refit the dust cap and proceed to the next caliper in the correct sequence.

It is recommended that all fluid drained from the system be discarded and new fluid only used for topping up. However, if the drained fluid is new and perfectly clean, allow it to stand for at least 24 hours to ensure that it is free from air bubbles before re-use. Always store brake fluid in clean, sealed containers.

10:6 Handbrake linkage

Handbrake cable adjustment is described in **Section 10:2**.

Handbrake linkage components are shown in **FIG 10:12**. To renew a handbrake cable, fully release the handbrake and, if necessary, slacken the adjusting nut to release all tension from the cable. Disconnect the cable from equaliser and rear brake caliper and remove from beneath the car. Install the new cable, making sure that it passes correctly around the pulley, then carry out the adjustment procedure described in **Section 10:2**. Clean and lightly lubricate equaliser unit and cable pulleys.

10:7 Fault diagnosis

(a) Spongy pedal

1 Leak in the system
2 Worn master cylinder
3 Leaking caliper cylinder
4 Air in the fluid system

(b) Excessive pedal movement

1 Check 1 and 4 in (a)
2 Excessive wear of friction pads
3 Very low fluid level in supply reservoir

(c) Brakes grab or pull to one side

1 Distorted brake disc
2 Wet or oily friction pads
3 Loose caliper
4 Disc or hub loose
5 Worn suspension or steering connections
6 Mixed linings of different grades
7 Uneven tyre pressures
8 Seized handbrake caliper
9 Seized caliper piston

(d) Brakes partly or fully locked on

1 Swollen friction linings
2 Damaged brake pipes preventing fluid return
3 Master cylinder compensating hole blocked
4 Master cylinder piston seized
5 Pedal return spring broken
6 Dirt in the hydraulic system
7 Seized caliper piston
8 Seized handbrake mechanism

(e) Brake failure

1 Empty fluid reservoir
2 Broken hydraulic pipeline
3 Ruptured master cylinder seal
4 Ruptured caliper seal

(f) Reservoir empties too quickly

1 Leaks in pipelines
2 Deteriorated cylinder seals

(g) Pedal yields under continuous pressure

1 Faulty master cylinder seals
2 Faulty caliper seals
3 Leak in the system

NOTES

CHAPTER 11

THE ELECTRICAL SYSTEM

11:1 Description

All models covered by this manual have 12-volt electrical systems in which the negative terminal of the battery is earthed to the car bodywork.

There are wiring diagrams in **Technical Data** at the end of this manual which will enable those with electrical experience to trace and correct faults.

Some items of electrical equipment can be serviced to repair minor faults or renew worn components, but others can only be renewed complete if defective. In either case, items that are seriously defective, electrically or mechanically, should be replaced by new units, or reconditioned units which can be obtained on an exchange basis should be fitted.

11:2 The battery

To maintain the performance of the battery, it is essential to carry out the following operations, particularly in winter when heavy current demands must be met.

Keep the top and surrounding parts of the battery dry and clean, as dampness can cause current leakage. Clean off corrosion from the metal parts of the battery mounting with diluted ammonia and coat them with anti-sulphuric paint. Clean the terminal posts and smear them with petroleum jelly, tightening the terminal fixings securely. High electrical resistance due to corrosion of the battery terminals can be responsible for a lack of sufficient current to operate the starter motor.

Regularly check the electrolyte level in the battery cells and top up with distilled water, if necessary, to the correct level. Fill to the level mark on the case if one is provided, or follow the filling instructions printed on the battery or its cover. If neither case applies to the battery which is fitted, top up until the internal separators are just covered.

If a battery fault is suspected, test the condition of the cells with a hydrometer. Never add neat acid to the battery. If it is necessary to prepare new electrolyte due to loss or spillage, add sulphuric acid to distilled water. It is highly dangerous to add water to acid. It is safest to have the battery refilled with electrolyte by a service station, if it is necessary.

The indications from the hydrometer readings of the specific gravity are as follows:

For climates below 27°C (80°F)				Specific gravity
Cell fully charged..	..	..	..	1.270 to 1.290
Cell half discharged	..	..	..	1.190 to 1.210
Cell discharged ..	..	..	..	1.110 to 1.130

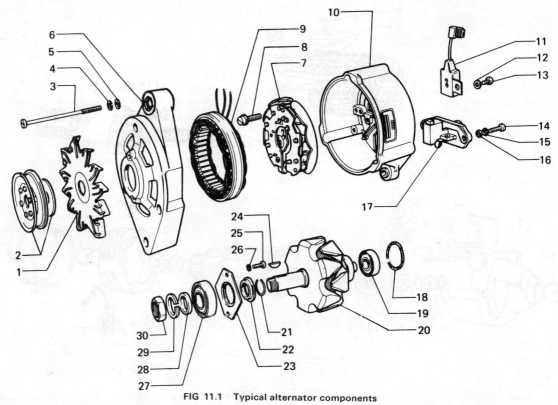

FIG 11.1 Typical alternator components

Key to Fig 11:1   1 Cooling fan   2 Pulley   3 Through bolt   4 Lockwasher   5 Washer   6 End bracket   7 Plate   8 Screw
9 Stator   10 Housing   11 Capacitor   12 Washer   13, 14 Screws   15 Lockwasher   16 Washer   17 Brush holder
18 Seal   19 Bearing   20 Rotor   21 Clip   22 Seal   23 Retainer   24 Key   25 Screw   26 Washer   27 Bearing
28 Seal   29 Lockwasher   30 Nut

For climates above 27°C (80°F)

Cell fully charged..	..	..	..	1.210 to 1.230
Cell half discharged	..	..	..	1.130 to 1.150
Cell discharged ..	..	..	..	1.030 to 1.070

These figures assume an electrolyte temperature of 16°C (60°F). If the temperature exceeds this, add 0.002 to the readings for each 3°C (5°F) rise. Subtract 0.002 for any corresponding drop below the stated temperature.

If the battery is in a low state of charge, take the car for a long daylight run or put the battery on a charger at 5 amps, until it gases freely. If an auto-fill type of battery is installed, the battery cover should be left in place during charging to prevent loss of electrolyte. If the battery is fitted with screw caps, these should be removed during charging. Do not use a naked light near the battery as the gas is inflammable. If the battery is to stand unused for long periods, give a refreshing charge every month. It will be ruined if it is left in a discharged state. Always disconnect the battery from the car electrical system when it is being charged from an outside source, to prevent damage to alternator internal components.

11:3 The alternator

The alternator provides current for the various items of electrical equipment and to charge the battery, the unit operating at all engine speeds. The current produced is alternate, this being rectified to direct current supply by diodes mounted in the alternator casing. Alternator drive is by belt from the crankshaft pulley. Very little maintenance is needed, apart from the occasional check on belt tension as described later, and on the condition and security of wiring connections.

The alternator must never be run with the battery disconnected, nor must the battery cables be reversed at any time. Test connections must be carefully made, and the battery and alternator must be completely disconnected before any electric welding is carried out on any part of the car. The engine must never be started with a battery charger still connected to the battery, although it is in order to use a second, fully charged battery to boost the one in the car in order to start the engine. In the latter case, make sure that the jump leads are connected positive to positive and negative to negative. These warnings must be observed, otherwise extensive damage to the alternator components, particularly the diodes, will result.

The alternator is designed and constructed to provide many years of trouble free service. If a fault should develop in the unit, it should be checked and serviced by a fully equipped service station or a reconditioned unit obtained and fitted.

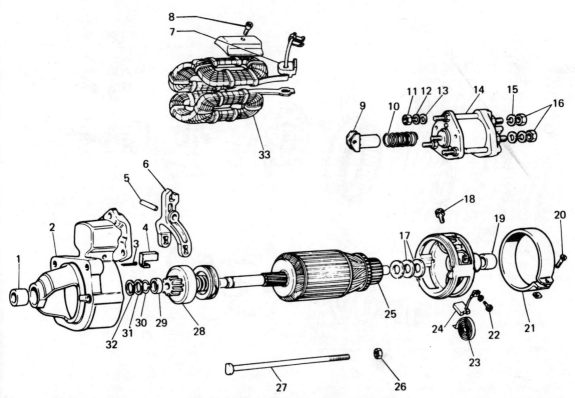

FIG 11:2   Typical starter motor components

Key to Fig 11:2   1 Bush   2 End bracket   3 Cotter pin   4 Rubber block   5 Pivot pin   6 Engagement lever   7 Insulator
8 Screw   9 Plunger   10 Spring   11 Nut   12 Lockwasher   13 Washer   14 Solenoid   15 Lockwasher   16 Nut
17 Washers   18 Screw   19 Bush   20 Screw   21 Cover   22 Screw   23 Brush spring   24 Carbon brush   25 Armature
26 Nut   27 Bolt   28 Drive pinion assembly   29 Stop ring   30 Circlip   31, 32 Washers   33 Field coils

Checking alternator operation:

A simple check on alternator charging can be carried out after dark by switching on the headlamps and starting the engine. If the alternator is charging, the headlamps will brighten considerably as the system voltage rises from the nominal battery voltage to the higher figure produced by the alternator.

If the alternator is not charging, check the wiring and connections in the charging circuit, then check the brush gear as described later. If these are in order, the alternator or regulator is at fault, so checks and any necessary repairs should be carried out by a service station.

Carbon brush renewal:

This work can be carried out without the need for alternator removal. Disconnect the battery earth cable then disconnect the wiring from alternator. **FIG 11:1** shows typical alternator components. Remove brush holder 17, then remove and discard the old brushes. Clean the brush holder and install the new brushes.

The slip rings on rotor 20 on which the brushes operate should be cleaned with a petrol-moistened cloth. Hold the cloth through the brush holder mounting hole. To facilitate cleaning, slacken the drive belt as described in **Chapter 4**,

then remove the belt from the alternator pulley so that the pulley can be turned by hand.

On completion, refit the brush holder assembly, reconnect the wiring then reconnect battery earth cable. Reset belt tension as described in **Chapter 4**.

Alternator removal:

Disconnect the battery, then disconnect cables to the alternator. Slacken and remove the drive belt as described in **Chapter 4**. Unbolt and remove the alternator.

Refitting is a reversal of the removal procedure, adjusting belt tension as described in **Chapter 4**.

Alternator bearing removal:

Remove the alternator as described previously. Refer to **FIG 11:1**. Mark the relationships of end bracket 6 and housing 10 to maintain alignment when reassembling. Remove the securing nut, then remove pulley and washer 2 and cooling fan 1 from the shaft. Collect locating key 24.

Remove the three through bolts 3 and separate end bracket from housing. Hold the shaft of rotor 20 and carefully tap housing with a soft-faced hammer to remove the rotor. Remove the screws and detach bearing retainer 23, then remove the bearing assembly. Use a suitable

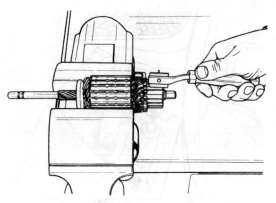

FIG 11:3 Undercutting commutator insulation

puller to remove rear bearing 19 from the rotor shaft. If the bearings are obviously defective, discard them, otherwise clean the bearings in a suitable solvent and check for wear or damage by rotating by hand. If faults are found the bearing should be renewed. Fit the bearings and reassemble the components in the reverse order of removal, using new bearing seals if the originals are not in good condition. The bearings should be lubricated with grease. Do not overlubricate and take care to avoid lubricant contamination of rotor slip rings or brush gear.

11:4 The starter motor

The starter is a brush type series wound motor equipped with an overrunning clutch and operated by a solenoid. The armature shaft is supported in metal bushes which require no routine servicing.

When the starter is operated from the switch, the engagement lever moves the pinion into mesh with the engine ring gear. When the pinion meshes with the ring gear teeth, the solenoid contact closes the circuit and the starter motor operates to turn the engine. When the engine starts, the speed of the rotating ring gear causes the pinion to overrun the clutch and armature. The pinion continues in engagement until the switch is released, when the engagement lever returns it to the rest position under spring pressure.

On models so equipped, the seat belt interlock system prevents current from reaching the starter solenoid, thereby preventing starter operation, unless the seat belts are correctly fastened.

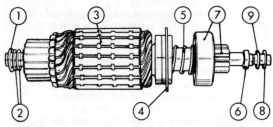

FIG 11:4 Armature and drive pinion assembly

Key to Fig 11:4   1 Thrust washer   2 Plain washers
3 Armature   4 Sleeve   5 Spring   6 Stop ring   7 Drive
pinion   8, 9 Plain washers

Tests for a starter which does not operate:

Check that the battery is in good condition and fully charged and that its connections are clean and tight. Switch on the headlamps and operate the starter switch. Current is reaching the starter if the lights dim when the starter is operated, in which case it will be necessary to remove the starter for servicing. If the lights do not dim significantly, switch them off and operate the starter switch while listening for a clicking sound at the starter motor, which will indicate that the starter solenoid is operating. If no sound can be heard at the starter when the switch is operated, check the wiring and connections between the battery and the starter switch, and between the switch and the solenoid. If a seat belt interlock system is incorporated, use a test lamp to check for current supply to the solenoid feed terminal while the ignition switch is turned to the starting position. If no current is available, either the wiring or connections are defective as just described, or there is a fault in the interlock system which should be checked and repaired at a service station.

If the solenoid can be heard operating when the starter switch is operated, check the wiring and connections between the battery and the main starter motor terminal, taking care not to accidentally earth the main battery to starter motor lead which is live at all times. If the wiring is not the cause of the trouble, the fault is internal and the starter motor must be removed and serviced.

Removing the starter:

Disconnect the battery then disconnect the wiring from starter to motor terminals. Remove the three fixing screws securing the starter to the engine block, then withdraw the unit by sliding it horizontally from its mountings.

Refitting is a reversal of this procedure.

Dismantling starter motor:

FIG 11:2 shows starter motor internal components. Remove the nut and detach the terminal which connects solenoid to starter motor, then remove nuts 11 and detach solenoid 14. Slacken screw 20 and remove cover 21. Remove screws 22 securing brush terminals, then release springs 23 and lift brushes 24 slightly in their holders. Position springs against sides of brushes to hold them in this position, then remove the screws securing brush holder assembly and detach from starter body. Collect thrust washers. Remove nuts 26 on through bolts 27, then remove starter body from end bracket 2. Remove cotter pin 3 and pivot pin 5, then pull armature assembly 25 from end bracket. Note location of rubber block 4.

Servicing components:
Cleaning:

Blow away all loose dust and dirt with an air-line. Use a small brush to clean out crevices. Petrol or methylated spirits may be used to help in cleaning the metal parts, but the field coils, armature and drive pinion assembly must under no circumstances be soaked with solvent.

Brush gear:

Check the brushes for wear or contamination. Clean the brushes and holders with a petrol-moistened cloth and check that the brushes move freely in their holders. If a brush sticks, ease the sides of the brush by polishing with a smooth file. If any brush is excessively worn or damaged in any way, all brushes should be renewed as a set.

The commutator:

The commutator on which the carbon brushes operate should have a smooth polished surface which is dark in appearance. Wiping over with a piece of cloth moistened with methylated spirits or petrol is usually sufficient to clean the surface. Light burn marks or scores can be polished off with fine grade glass paper (do not use emery cloth as this leaves particles embedded in the copper). Deeper damage may be skimmed off in a lathe, at high speed and using a very sharp tool. A diamond-tipped tool should be used for a light final cut. On completion, the mica between commutator segments must be undercut to a minimum depth of 1.0mm (0.04in), using a special tool as shown in **FIG 11:3** or a hacksaw blade ground to the width of the insulation. Make sure that all dust is cleaned from the commutator when the work is complete.

The armature:

Check the armature for charred insulation, loose segments or laminations and for scored laminations. Short circuited windings may be suspected if individual commutator segments are badly burned. If the armature is damaged in any way it should be renewed. If an electrical fault in the armature is suspected, have it tested on special equipment at a service station.

Field coils:

The field coils and pole pieces are held in place by special screws. To ensure correct installation and alignment it is recommended that field coil checking and servicing be carried out at a service station.

The field coils can be checked for continuity using a test lamp and battery. A better method is to check the resistance using an ohmmeter. The resistance can also be checked using a 12-volt battery and ammeter (voltage divided by a current equals resistance).

Bearings:

If the bearing bushes are excessively worn, they should be renewed at a service station, as press equipment and very accurate mandrels are required to install the new bushes. If the bearings are in good condition, they should be lightly lubricated with engine oil during reassembly.

Drive pinion assembly:

The starter drive pinion and clutch assembly must not be washed in solvents, as this would wash away the internal lubricant. Cleaning should be confined to wiping away dirt with a cloth. Light damage to the pinion teeth which engage the engine ring gear can be cleaned off with a fine file or oilstone, deeper damage necessitates the renewal of the complete drive assembly. Check that the clutch takes up the drive instantaneously but slips freely in the opposite direction. The complete assembly must be renewed if the clutch is defective.

To remove the starter drive, refer to **FIG 11:4** and use a suitable piece of metal tube to drive the stop ring 6 down the shaft to free the circlip, then remove the circlip and pull

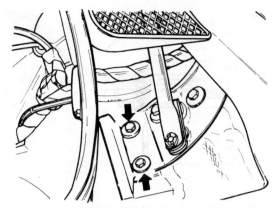

FIG 11:5   Wiper motor removal

off the stop ring and drive pinion assembly. Refit in the reverse order of removal, making sure that the stop ring is pulled over the circlip to retain it securely.

Reassembly:

This is a reversal of the removal procedure. Lubricate the bearing bushes and the splines on the starter drive assembly with a thin coating of engine oil and the face of stop ring for drive pinion with lithium based grease. Do not over-lubricate and take care not to contaminate commutator, brush gear or electrical winding with lubricant.

11:5 Fuses

The fuses which protect the main electrical circuits are mounted in a fusebox situated beneath the instrument panel and provided with a snap-on cover.

If a fuse blows, briefly check the circuit that it protects and install a new fuse. Check each circuit in turn and if the new fuse does not blow, it is likely that the old one had weakened with age. If the new fuse blows, carefully check the circuit that was live at the time and do not fit another fuse until the fault has been found and repaired. A fuse that blows intermittently will make it more difficult to correct the fault, but try shaking the wiring loom, as the fault is likely to be caused by chafed insulation making intermittent contact.

Never fit a fuse of higher rating than that specified, and never use anything as a substitute for a fuse of the correct type. The fuse is designed to be the weak link in the circuit and if a higher rated fuse or an incorrect substitute is installed the wiring may fail instead.

11:6 Windscreen wipers

The windscreen wipers are operated by a two-speed electric motor incorporating a self-parking switch.

If wiper operation is sluggish, check the linkage for binding. If the motor is inoperative, check the fuse first, then check the wiring and connections between the battery and switch and between the switch and wiper motor. If the motor unit is defective, a new or exchange unit should be obtained and fitted.

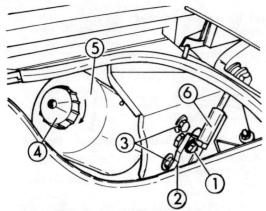

FIG 11:6   Headlamp motor removal

Key to Fig 11:6   1 Bolt   2 Arm   3 Bolts   4 Cap
5 Motor   6 Adjuster for headlamp vertical alignment

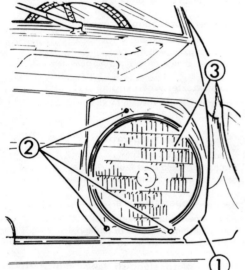

FIG 11:7   Headlamp unit removal

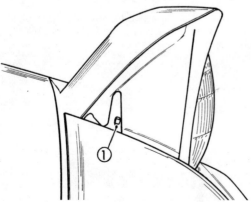

FIG 11:8   Headlamp horizontal adjustment screw

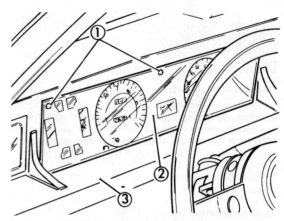

FIG 11:9   Instrument panel removal

Wiper motor removal:

Remove the wiper arms by carefully levering the mountings from splined shafts. Open the front compartment lid, then disconnect the wiper wiring connector. Remove the two bolts shown in **FIG 11:5**, then unscrew the nut which attaches linkage to wiper motor arm. Separate linkage from motor and remove the motor. Operate linkage by hand to check for wear or binding and renew parts if necessary.

Install the motor in the reverse order of removal, lubricating linkage joints with waterproof grease. On completion, use the screenwasher or plain water to wet the screen, then check wiper operation. If the sweep area of any wiper is incorrect, or if a wiper blade contacts the screen surround at any point, reposition the arm on the shaft as necessary.

11:7 Headlamps

If the motors fail to raise or lower the headlamp units, check the fuses first. If these are in order, check the wiring and connections in the operating circuit. If a motor is faulty a new or exchange unit should be obtained and fitted.

Care should be taken when working on the headlamp units, for if the battery is not disconnected slight movement may start the motor and the fingers may be trapped in the mechanism.

Headlamp motor removal:

Refer to **FIG 11:6**. Take care not to turn cap 4, otherwise the motor, if operative, will retract the headlamp unit. Remove bolt 1 securing arm 2 to motor shaft. Remove three bolts and washers 3 securing motor 5, then disconnect the electrical connector and remove the motor.

Refit in the reverse order of removal, making sure that motor earth wire is fitted under the appropriate mounting bolt 3. On completion, it is recommended that headlamp beam setting be checked as described later.

Headlamp unit removal:

Refer to **FIG 11:7**. Remove the three screws securing frame 1 to body, then remove the frame. Loosen the three screws 2 securing headlamp ring, then turn ring to left and remove. Remove plug from rear of headlamp unit 3, then remove the unit.

Installation is a reversal of the removal procedure. On completion, it is recommended that headlamp beam setting be checked as described next.

Headlamp beam setting:

Headlamp beam setting is carried out by slackening the locknuts and turning adjuster shown at 6 in **FIG 11:6** for vertical adjustment and by turning the screw shown at 1 in **FIG 11:8** for horizontal adjustment. The car must be unladen and the tyres correctly inflated when adjustments are carried out. The work is best carried out by a service station having special optical equipment, in order to achieve accurate results.

11:8 Instrument panel

Removal:

Refer to **FIG 11:9**. Disconnect the battery to prevent accidental short circuits, then remove five screws 1 securing instrument panel 2 to facia 3. Pull the panel out slightly, then reach behind it and disconnect the three electrical connectors and the speedometer cable. Remove the instrument panel from the facia.

Refitting is a reversal of the removal procedure. On completion, reconnect the battery then check operation of instruments, gauges and warning lights.

11:9 Fault diagnosis

(a) Battery discharged

1 Terminal connections loose or dirty
2 Shorts in lighting circuits
3 Alternator not charging
4 Regulator faulty
5 Battery internally defective

(b) Insufficient charge rate

1 Check 1 and 4 in (a)
2 Drive belt slipping
3 Alternator defective

(c) Battery will not hold charge

1 Low electrolyte level
2 Electrolyte leakage from cracked case
3 Battery internally defective

(d) Battery overcharged

1 Regulator faulty

(e) Alternator output low or nil

1 Drive belt broken or slipping
2 Regulator faulty
3 Brushes sticking, springs weak or broken
4 Faulty internal windings
5 Defective diode(s)

(f) Starter motor lacks power or will not turn

1 Battery discharged, loose cable connections
2 Starter switch or solenoid faulty
3 Brushes worn or sticking, leads detached or shorting
4 Commutator dirty or worn
5 Starter shaft bent
6 Engine abnormally stiff

(g) Starter runs but does not turn engine

1 Pinion engagement mechanism faulty
2 Broken teeth on pinion or engine ring gear

(h) Starter motor rough or noisy

1 Mounting bolts loose
2 Pinion engagement mechanism faulty
3 Damaged pinion or engine ring gear teeth

(j) Noisy starter when engine is running

1 Pinion return mechanism faulty
2 Mounting bolts loose

(k) Starter motor inoperative

1 Check 1, 2 and 3 in (f)
2 Armature or field coils faulty
3 Seat belt interlock circuit faulty (where fitted)

(l) Lamps inoperative or erratic

1 Battery low, bulbs burned out
2 Faulty earthing of lamps or battery
3 Lighting switch faulty, loose or broken connections

(m) Wiper motor sluggish, taking high current

1 Wiper motor internally defective
2 Wiper motor fixings loose
3 Linkage worn or binding

NOTES

CHAPTER 12

THE BODYWORK

12:1 Bodywork finish

Large scale repairs to body panels are best left to expert panel beaters. Even small dents can be tricky, too much hammering will stretch the metal and make things worse instead of better. If panel beating is to be attempted, use a dolly on the opposite side of the panel. The head of a large hammer will suffice for small dents, but for large dents, a block of metal will be necessary. Use light hammer blows to reshape the panel, pressing the dolly against the opposite side of the panel to absorb the blows. If this method is used to reduce the depth of dents, final smoothing with a suitable filler will be easier, although it may be better to avoid hammering minor dents and just use the filler.

Clean the area to be filled, making sure that it is free from paint, rust and grease, then roughen the area with emerycloth to ensure a good bond. Use a proprietary fibreglass filler paste mixed according to the manufacturer's instructions and press it into the dent with a putty knife or similar flat-bladed tool. Allow the filler to stand proud of the surrounding area to allow for rubbing down after hardening. Use a file and emerycloth or a disc sander to blend the repaired area to the surrounding bodywork, using finer grade abrasive as the work nears completion. Apply a coat of primer surfacer and, when it is

dry, rub down with 'Wet or Dry' paper lubricated with soapy water, finishing with 400 grade. Apply more primer and repeat the operation until the surface is perfectly smooth. Take time on achieving the best finish possible at this stage as it will control the final effect.

The touching-up of paintwork can be carried out with self-spraying cans of paint, these being available in a wide range of colours. Use a piece of newspaper or board as a test panel to practise on first, so that the action of the spray will be familiar when it is used on the panel. Before spraying the panel, remove all traces of wax polish. Mask off large areas such as windows with newspaper and masking tape. Small areas such as trim strips or door handles can be wrapped with masking tape or carefully coated with grease or Vaseline. Apply the touching-up paint, spraying with short bursts and keeping the spray moving. Do not attempt to cover the area in one coat, applying several coats with a few minutes' drying time between each. If too much paint is applied at one time, runs may develop. If so, do not try to remove the run by wiping but wait until it is dry and rub down as before.

After the final coat has been applied, allow a few hours of drying time before blending the new finish to the old with fine cutting compound, buffing with a light, circular motion. Finish with the application of a good quality polish.

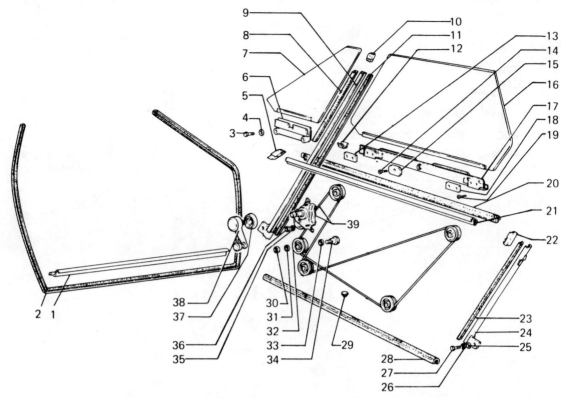

FIG 12:1 Door glass and regulator mechanism components

Key to Fig 12:1 1 Doorsill moulding 2 Weatherstrip 3 Bolt 4 Washer 5 Boot 6 Channel 7 Glass 8 Weatherstrip
9 Pillar 10 Pad 11 Weatherstrip 12 Clip 13 Plate 14 Screw 15 Pad 16 Glass 17 Guide 18 Plate 19 Screw
20 Weatherstrip 21 Cover 22 Boot 23 Weatherstrip 24 Channel 25 Washer 26 Lockwasher 27 Screw
28 Weatherstrip 29 Pad 30 Nut 31 Washer 32 Pulley 33 Washer 34 Bolt 35 Lockwasher 36 Nut 37 Bezel
38 Handle 39 Window regulator

12:2 Door components

Door window glass and regulator mechanism components are shown in **FIG 12:1**, door lock and operating mechanism components in **FIG 12:2**.

Door trim panel removal:

Refer to **FIG 12:3**. Carefully lever plug 1 from armrest 2, then remove three screws and detach armrest from door. Remove screw and lock operating handle 4. Unscrew and remove lock button 3 from lockrod. Lever cover 5 away from handle 6 and push the handle towards the regulator to remove. Carefully lever the trim panel 7 from door inner panel to release the retaining clips, using a large screwdriver or suitable flat-bladed tool.

Refitting is a reversal of the removal procedure.

Window glass adjustment:

Remove the trim panel as described previously. Wind the window glass down fully, then refer to **FIG 12:1**. Slacken the screws securing clamp plates 13 and 18, then allow the window to rest on the rubber pad provided. In this position firmly retighten the clamp plate screws. Check that the glass can be operated smoothly through its

full range of movement and that the control cable winds and unwinds properly on the regulator pulley. If necessary, make further fine adjustments to correct any faults.

Regulator cable tensioning:

If the regulator cable slackens in service and slips on the pulleys, retension in the following manner:

Remove the trim panel as described previously. Refer to **FIG 12:4** and loosen nut 2 securing idler pulley. Move idler pulley in slot 3 until tension of cable 1 is correct, then firmly retighten nut. Check operation of window through full range of movement.

Door lock adjustment:

If the door lock does not operate correctly from the outside handle, remove the trim panel as described previously and disconnect the upper end of rod shown at 24 in **FIG 12:2**. Rotate the connector as necessary to modify the length of the rod, temporarily reconnecting and checking after each adjustment. When correct, reconnect and secure the rod then refit the trim panel.

If the lock does not operate correctly from the inside handle, remove the trim panel as described previously then

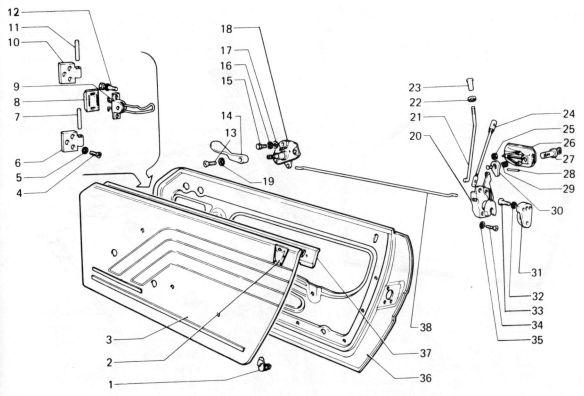

FIG 12:2 Door lock and operating mechanism components

Key to Fig 12:2   1 Clip   2 Lock cover   3 Door trim panel   4 Screw   5 Lockwasher   6 Hinge half   7 Pin   8 Lining
9 Door check   10 Hinge half   11 Pin   12 Bolt   13 Screw   14 Handle   15 Bolt   16 Lockwasher   17 Washer
18 Lever   19 Lockwasher   20 Lock   21 Rod   22 Rubber ring   23 Knob   24 Rod   25 Nut   26 Handle   27 Lock
cylinder   28 Pin   29 Spring   30 Pawl   31 Striker plate   32 Lockwasher   33, 34 Screws   35 Lockwasher   36 Door
37 Channel   38 Rod

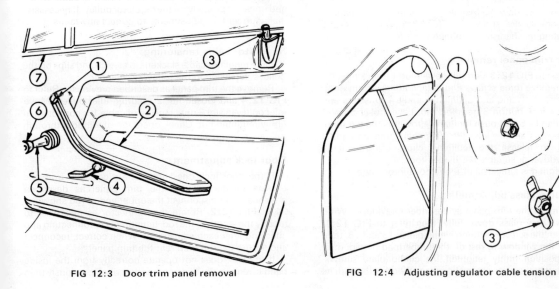

FIG 12:3   Door trim panel removal   FIG   12:4   Adjusting regulator cable tension

FIG 12:5 Door lock striker adjustment

slacken the screws 15 securing lock 18 to door panel (see **FIG 12:2**). Move the lock as necessary within the range allowed by the mounting holes, then retighten the bolts and refit the trim panel.

If a door does not close fully when shut or needs excessive slamming to close fully, the position of the lock striker plate can be modified to cure the fault. Refer to **FIG 12:5**. Scribe around the striker plate so that its original position is known, then slacken screws 2 and move plate 1 in or out as necessary. Firmly retighten the screws, then check that the door closes correctly. Note that it is essential for the door to close with two distinct clicks, in the safety catch and fully locked position. The striker plate must never be adjusted so that the door closes in the safety catch position only.

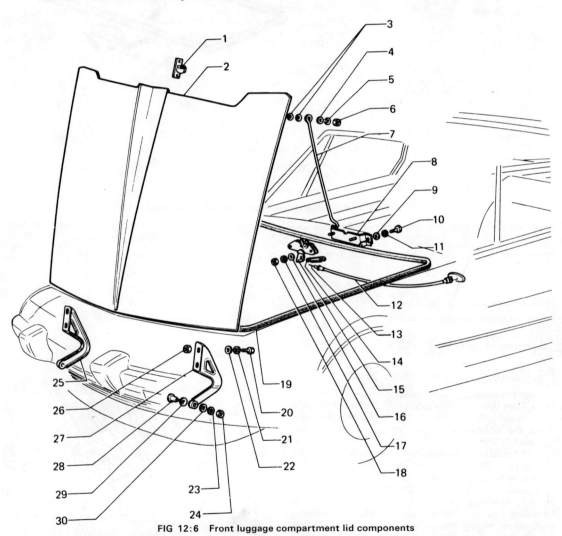

FIG 12:6 Front luggage compartment lid components

Key to Fig 12:6   1 Striker plate   2 Lid   3 Spring washers   4 Washers   5 Lockwasher   6 Nut   7 Rod   8 Lock bracket
9 Washers   10 Bolt   11 Washer   12 Outer sleeve   13 Lock cable   14 Spring   15 Lock   16 Washer   17 Lockwasher
18 Nut   19 Compartment rubber seal   20 Bolt   21 Lockwasher   22 Washer   23 Lockwasher   24 Nut   25 Hinge
26 Nut   27 Hinge   28 Bolt   29, 30 Washers

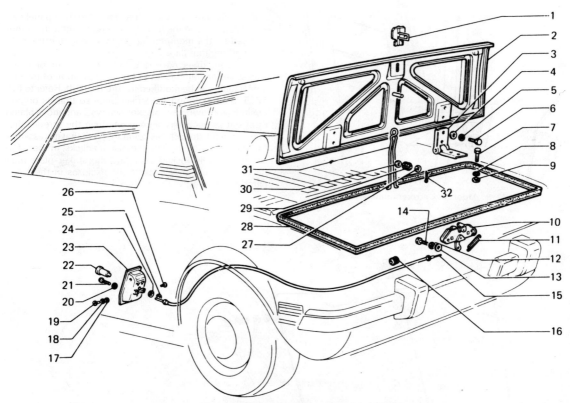

FIG 12:7   Rear luggage compartment lid components

Key to Fig 12:7   1 Striker plate   **2** Lid   **3** Hinge   **4** Washer   **5** Lockwasher   **6, 7** Bolts   **8** Lockwasher   **9** Washer
10 Lock   **11** Spring   **12** Lockwasher   **13** Washer   **14** Bolt   **15** Cable   **16** Rubber ring   **17** Washer   **18** Lockwasher
19 Screw   **20** Lockwasher   **21** Screw   **22** Lock cylinder   **23** Handle   **24** Washer   **25** Fork   **26** Screw   **27** Washer
28 Weatherstrip   **29** Bushing   **30** Washer   **31** Stay

12:3 Engine and luggage compartment lids

Front luggage compartment lid:

Front luggage compartment lid, hinge and lock components are shown in **FIG 12:6**.

Lid removal:

Raise the lid and scribe the hinge positions on the panel to facilitate refitting. Disconnect stay 7 from lid. Slacken the four bolts 20, then have an assistant steady the panel while the bolts, lockwashers and plain washers are removed. Lift off the lid.

Refit the lid in the reverse order of removal, aligning the hinges with the scribe marks previously made before tightening the bolts. Close the lid and check for a correct fit. If misalignment is evident, slacken the retaining bolts again sufficiently to allow the panel to be moved on the hinges, re-align as necessary, then retighten the bolts.

If, when closed, the panel is above the adjacent bodywork at the rear, or if the bonnet closes too tightly, slacken the lock retaining bolts and move the lock assembly slightly to correct. Tighten the bolts firmly on completion.

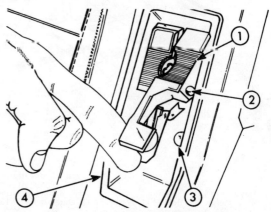

FIG 12:8   Cable operating lever removal

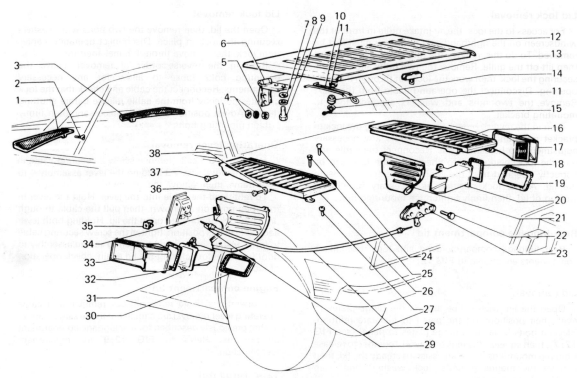

FIG 12:9   Engine compartment lid and air inlets

Key to Fig 12:9   1 Grille   2 Screw   3 Grille   4 Washers   5 Nut   6 Hinge   7 Washer   8 Lock washer   9 Bolt
10 Stay   11 Washer   12 Lid   13 Striker plate   14 Bushing   15 Cotter pin   16 Grille   17 Conveyor   18, 19 Gaskets
20, 21 Ducts   22 Bolt   23 Lock   24, 25 Screws   26 Grille   27 Screw   28 Outer sleeve   29 Lock cable   30 Gasket
31 Duct   32 Gasket   33 Air intake   34 Duct   35 Clip   36, 37 Screws   38 Washer

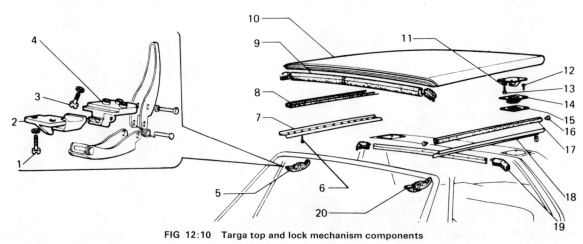

FIG 12:10   Targa top and lock mechanism components

Key to Fig 12:10   1 Screw   2 Striker plate   3 Screw   4 Support   5 Lock   6 Screw   7 Moulding   8, 9 Weatherstrips
10 Targa top   11 Lug   12, 13 Screws   14 Striker plate   15 Covering   16 Plug   17 Weatherstrip   18 Moulding
19 Joint   20 Lock

Lid lock removal:

For access to the lock, the air intake grille in front of the windscreen on the righthand side of the car must first be removed. To do this, remove the four screws and the bolt then lift off the grille. Remove the two bolts and washers securing the lock, then work the lock out through the grille opening. Disconnect the operating cable from the lock. Remove the two nuts and washers securing lock to mounting bracket.

Refit in the reverse order of removal, leaving the lock to bracket mounting bolts loose to enable any necessary adjustments to be carried out. Reconnect the cable and refit the lock, being sure to check that the lock can be correctly operated from the cable release before closing the lid. Adjust lock position as necessary for correct closing of lid, then firmly tighten the mounting bolts.

Rear luggage compartment lid:

Rear luggage compartment lid and lock mechanism components are shown in **FIG 12:7**.

Lid removal:

Open the lid, then scribe around the hinge plates to mark their positions on the panel to facilitate refitting. Slacken bolts 6 securing hinge plates to panel (see **FIG 12:7**), then squeeze the legs of stay 31 together to release from the mountings. Have an assistant steady the lid, then remove the mounting bolts, lock washers and plain washers and remove the lid.

Refit in the reverse order of removal, aligning the scribe marks previously made. If the lid is not correctly aligned in the aperture, slacken the hinge securing bolts and move the lid as necessary before retightening the bolts. If when locked the lid is too tight or too loose, slacken the lock mounting bolts, move the lock as necessary, then retighten the bolts.

Lid lock removal:

Open the lid, then remove the two bolts with washers securing the lock in place. Disconnect operating cables from lock, then remove through panel aperture.

Refit in the reverse order of removal. Leave the mounting bolts loose to allow for any necessary adjustments. Reconnect the cable and check that the lock operates correctly from the cable release before shutting the lid. Adjust position of lock as necessary, then firmly tighten mounting bolts.

Operating lever removal:

Refer to **FIG 12:8**. Remove screw 2 securing cable in lever 1. Remove screw 3 holding the lever assembly 4 to door frame, then remove the assembly.

To refit, feed the cable into the lever. Hold the lever in the open position as shown, then pull the cable through until the lock operates to open the lid. Holding both lever and cable in this position, tighten the screw securing cable to lever. Install screw 3 and tighten to secure assembly to door frame. Before closing the lid again, check operation of lock.

Engine compartment lid:

The operations of lid removal, lock removal and cable operating lever removal are carried out in the same manner as that previously described for rear luggage compartment components. Refer to **FIG 12:9** for component identification.

12:4 Targa top

Removal of targa top lock mechanism and related components is a straightforward operation, referring to **FIG 12:10** for component identification. If the top is misaligned when fitted and locked, adjust with the top open by slackening screws 1 securing striker plate 2, moving the striker plate as necessary then firmly retightening the screws.

NOTES

NOTES

APPENDIX

TECHNICAL DATA

Engine   Fuel system   Ignition system   Cooling system
Transmission   Suspension   Steering   Brakes
Electrical system   Tightening torques   Wiring diagrams

HINTS ON MAINTENANCE AND OVERHAUL

GLOSSARY OF TERMS

INDEX

Inches	Decimals	Milli-metres	Inches to Millimetres		Millimetres to Inches	
			Inches	mm	mm	Inches
1/64	.015625	.3969	.001	.0254	.01	.00039
1/32	.03125	.7937	.002	.0508	.02	.00079
3/64	.046875	1.1906	.003	.0762	.03	.00118
1/16	.0625	1.5875	.004	.1016	.04	.00157
5/64	.078125	1.9844	.005	.1270	.05	.00197
3/32	.09375	2.3812	.006	.1524	.06	.00236
7/64	.109375	2.7781	.007	.1778	.07	.00276
1/8	.125	3.1750	.008	.2032	.08	.00315
9/64	.140625	3.5719	.009	.2286	.09	.00354
5/32	.15625	3.9687	.01	.254	.1	.00394
11/64	.171875	4.3656	.02	.508	.2	.00787
3/16	.1875	4.7625	.03	.762	.3	.01181
13/64	.203125	5·1594	.04	1.016	.4	.01575
7/32	.21875	5.5562	.05	1.270	.5	.01969
15/64	.234375	5.9531	.06	1.524	.6	.02362
1/4	.25	6.3500	.07	1.778	.7	.02756
17/64	.265625	6.7469	.08	2.032	.8	.03150
9/32	.28125	7.1437	.09	2.286	.9	.03543
19/64	.296875	7.5406	.1	2.54	1	.03937
5/16	.3125	7.9375	.2	5.08	2	.07874
21/64	.328125	8.3344	.3	7.62	3	.11811
11/32	.34375	8.7312	.4	10.16	4	.15748
23/64	.359375	9.1281	.5	12.70	5	.19685
3/8	.375	9.5250	.6	15.24	6	.23622
25/64	.390625	9.9219	.7	17.78	7	.27559
13/32	.40625	10.3187	.8	20.32	8	.31496
27/64	.421875	10.7156	.9	22.86	9	.35433
7/16	.4375	11.1125	1	25.4	10	.39370
29/64	.453125	11.5094	2	50.8	11	.43307
15/32	.46875	11.9062	3	76.2	12	.47244
31/64	.484375	12.3031	4	101.6	13	.51181
1/2	.5	12.7000	5	127.0	14	.55118
33/64	.515625	13.0969	6	152.4	15	.59055
17/32	.53125	13.4937	7	177.8	16	.62992
35/64	.546875	13.8906	8	203.2	17	.66929
9/16	.5625	14.2875	9	228.6	18	.70866
37/64	.578125	14.6844	10	254.0	19	.74803
19/32	.59375	15.0812	11	279.4	20	.78740
39/64	.609375	15.4781	12	304.8	21	.82677
5/8	.625	15.8750	13	330.2	22	.86614
41/64	.640625	16.2719	14	355.6	23	.90551
21/32	.65625	16.6687	15	381.0	24	.94488
43/64	.671875	17.0656	16	406.4	25	.98425
11/16	.6875	17.4625	17	431.8	26	1.02362
45/64	.703125	17.8594	18	457.2	27	1.06299
23/32	.71875	18.2562	19	482.6	28	1.10236
47/64	.734375	18.6531	20	508.0	29	1.14173
3/4	.75	19.0500	21	533.4	30	1.18110
49/64	.765625	19.4469	22	558.8	31	1.22047
25/32	.78125	19.8437	23	584.2	32	1.25984
51/64	.796875	20.2406	24	609.6	33	1.29921
13/16	.8125	20.6375	25	635.0	34	1.33858
53/64	.828125	21.0344	26	660.4	35	1.37795
27/32	.84375	21.4312	27	685.8	36	1.41732
55/64	.859375	21.8281	28	711.2	37	1.4567
7/8	.875	22.2250	29	736.6	38	1.4961
57/64	.890625	22.6219	30	762.0	39	1.5354
29/32	.90625	23.0187	31	787.4	40	1.5748
59/64	.921875	23.4156	32	812.8	41	1.6142
15/16	.9375	23.8125	33	838.2	42	1.6535
61/64	.953125	24.2094	34	863.6	43	1.6929
31/32	.96875	24.6062	35	889.0	44	1.7323
63/64	.984375	25.0031	36	914.4	45	1.7717

UNITS	Pints to Litres	Gallons to Litres	Litres to Pints	Litres to Gallons	Miles to Kilometres	Kilometres to Miles	Lbs. per sq. In. to Kg. per sq. Cm.	Kg. per sq. Cm. to Lbs. per sq. In.
1	.57	4.55	1.76	.22	1.61	.62	.07	14.22
2	1.14	9.09	3.52	.44	3.22	1.24	.14	28.50
3	1.70	13.64	5.28	.66	4.83	1.86	.21	42.67
4	2.27	18.18	7.04	.88	6.44	2.49	.28	56.89
5	2.84	22.73	8.80	1.10	8.05	3.11	.35	71.12
6	3.41	27.28	10.56	1.32	9.66	3.73	.42	85.34
7	3.98	31.82	12.32	1.54	11.27	4.35	.49	99.56
8	4.55	36.37	14.08	1.76	12.88	4.97	.56	113.79
9		40.91	15.84	1.98	14.48	5.59	.63	128.00
10		45.46	17.60	2.20	16.09	6.21	.70	142.23
20				4.40	32.19	12.43	1.41	284.47
30				6.60	48.28	18.64	2.11	426.70
40				8.80	64.37	24.85		
50					80.47	31.07		
60					96.56	37.28		
70					112.65	43.50		
80					128.75	49.71		
90					144.84	55.92		
100					160.93	62.14		

UNITS	Lb ft to kgm	Kgm to lb ft	UNITS	Lb ft to kgm	Kgm to lb ft
1	.138	7.233	7	.967	50.631
2	.276	14.466	8	1.106	57.864
3	.414	21.699	9	1.244	65.097
4	.553	28.932	10	1.382	72.330
5	.691	36.165	20	2.765	144.660
6	.829	43.398	30	4.147	216.990

TECHNICAL DATA

Dimensions are in inches with metric equivalents in brackets, unless otherwise stated

ENGINE

Capacity	78.70cu in (1290cc)
Bore and stroke	3.386 × 2.185 (86 × 55.5)

Compression ratio:
European models	8.9:1
USA models	8.5:1

Maximum bhp at rev/min:
European models	75 at 6000
USA models:	
1974	66.5 at 6000
1975-76	61 at 5800
1977 on	61.5 at 5800

Maximum torque at rev/min:
European models	71.6lb ft (9.9kgm) at 3400
USA models	67lb ft (9.3kgm) at 4000

Cylinder block and connecting rods:
Cylinder bore diameter (graded)	3.3858 to 3.3878 (86.000 to 86.050)
Auxiliary shaft bushes finished diameters:	
Drive end	1.4041 to 1.4049 (35.664 to 35.684)
Inside end	1.2598 to 1.2606 (32.000 to 32.020)
Main bearing seat diameter	2.1459 to 2.1465 (54.507 to 54.520)
Main bearing seat length between thrust rings ..	0.8716 to 0.8740 (22.140 to 22.200)
Big-end bearing housing diameter	1.9146 to 1.9152 (48.630 to 48.646)
Big-end bearing thickness:	
Standard	0.0603 to 0.0606 (1.531 to 1.538)
Undersize	0.010, 0.020, 0.030, 0.040 (0.254, 0.508, 0.762, 1.016)
Big-end bearing fit clearance	0.0014 to 0.0034 (0.036 to 0.086)
Small-end bore diameter	0.9425 to 0.9438 (23.939 to 23.972)
Small-end bushing outside diameter	0.9455 to 0.9465 (24.016 to 24.041)
Small-end bushing interference	0.0017 to 0.004 (0.044 to 0.102)
Small-end bushing ream bore:	
Grade 1	0.8663 to 0.8664 (22.004 to 22.007)
Grade 2	0.8664 to 0.8665 (22.007 to 22.010)
Piston pin fit clearance (new)	0.0004 to 0.0006 (0.010 to 0.016)
Maximum misalignment between connecting rod bearing centre lines 4.92 (125) from shank ..	0.0039 (0.10)

Pistons:
Diameter 1.35 (34.3) from crown:	
Class A	3.3835 to 3.3839 (85.940 to 85.950)
Class C	3.3842 to 3.3846 (85.960 to 85.970)
Class E	3.3850 to 3.3854 (85.980 to 85.990)
Oversizes	0.0079, 0.0157, 0.0236 (0.2, 0.4, 0.6)
Piston pin bore:	
Grade 1	0.8660 to 0.8661 (21.996 to 21.999)
Grade 2	0.8661 to 0.8662 (21.999 to 22.002)
Ring groove width:	
Top	0.0604 to 0.0612 (1.535 to 1.555)
Centre	0.0799 to 0.0807 (2.030 to 2.050)
Bottom	0.1562 to 0.1570 (3.967 to 3.987)

Piston pin diameter:
Grade 1	0.8658 to 0.8659 (21.991 to 21.994)
Grade 2	0.8659 to 0.8660 (21.994 to 21.997)
Oversize	0.0079 (0.2)

Piston pin clearance (new) .. .. .. : 0.0001 to 0.0003 (0.002 to 0.008)

Ring thickness:
Top, compression	0.0582 to 0.0587 (1.478 to 1.490)
Second, oil	0.0779 to 0.0783 (1.978 to 1.990)
Third, scraper	0.1545 to 0.1550 (3.925 to 3.937)

Ring side clearance (new):
Top	0.0018 to 0.0030 (0.045 to 0.077)
Second	0.0016 to 0.0028 (0.040 to 0.072)
Third	0.0012 to 0.0024 (0.030 to 0.062)

Ring gap (fitted):
Top and second	0.0118 to 0.0177 (0.30 to 0.45)
Third	0.0098 to 0.0157 (0.25 to 0.40)
Ring oversizes	0.0079, 0.0157, 0.0236 (0.2, 0.4, 0.6)

Piston clearance in bore 1.35 (34.3) from crown
and normal to pin, new parts .. .. .. : 0.0020 to 0.0028 (0.050 to 0.070)

Crankshaft and main bearings:
Main journal diameter (standard)	1.9994 to 2.0002 (50.785 to 50.805)
Main bearing seat bore	2.1459 to 2.1465 (54.507 to 54.520)
Main bearing thickness	0.0718 to 0.0721 (1.825 to 1.831)
Main bearing undersize	0.01, 0.02, 0.03, 0.04 (0.254, 0.508, 0.762, 1.016)
Crankpin diameter (standard)	1.7913 to 1.7920 (45.498 to 45.518)
Main bearing/journal clearance	0.0020 to 0.0037 (0.050 to 0.100)
Rear main journal length	1.062 to 1.0639 (26.975 to 27.025)
Rear main bearing width between thrust rings ..	0.8716 to 0.8740 (22.140 to 22.200)
Thrust ring thickness	0.0909 to 0.0929 (2.310 to 2.360)
Thrust ring oversizes	0.0959 to 0.0979 (2.437 to 2.487)
Thrust ring assembly clearance	0.0021 to 0.0104 (0.055 to 0.265)
Main journal eccentricity	0.0012 (0.03)
Main journal/crankpin misalignment ..	0.014 (0.35)
Main journal/crankpin maximum ovality ..	0.0002 (0.005) *
Main journal/crankpin maximum taper ..	0.0002 (0.005) *

* After grinding

Squareness of flywheel with crankshaft measured
1.344 (34) from centre line .. .. .. : 0.0010 (0.025)

Cylinder head:
Valve guide bore in head ..	0.5886 to 0.5896 (14.950 to 14.977)
Valve guide outside diameter	0.5913 to 0.5920 (15.018 to 15.036)
Valve guide inside diameter (fitted) ..	0.3158 to 0.3165 (8.022 to 8.040)

Valve seat inside diameter:
Inlet	1.1811 (30)
Exhaust	1.0433 (26.5)
Valve seat angle	45° ± 5'
Valve seat width	0.0787 (2)
Clearance between tappet and bore ..	0.0002 to 0.0020
Clearance between tappet and bore ..	0.0002 to 0.0020 (0.005 to 0.050)
Tappet cap plate (basic)	0.1575 ± 0.0004 (4 ± 0.01)
Cap plates supplied in thicknesses from ..	0.1279 to 0.1850
Cap plates supplied in thicknesses from ..	0.1279 to 0.1850 (3.25 to 4.70)
In increments of	0.0020 (0.051)

Valves:
Stem diameter:
- Inlet .. .. 0.3140 to 0.3146 (7.975 to 7.990)
- Exhaust .. .. 0.3142 to 0.3148 (7.980 to 7.995)

Head diameter:
- Inlet 1.4173 (36)
- Exhaust 1.2008 (30.5)

Maximum head eccentricity 0.0012 (0.03)
Head angle .. .. 45° 30′ ± 5′
Valve lift (without play) 0.3583 (9.1)

Clearance in guide:
- Inlet .. .. 0.0013 to 0.0026 (0.032 to 0.065)
- Exhaust .. .. 0.0011 to 0.0024 (0.027 to 0.060)

Valve springs:

	Inner	Outer
Height under load of 75.5lb (38.9kg)		1.417 (36)
Height under load of 32.7lb (14.9kg)	1.220 (31)	
Springs should be replaced when the above weights are produced by loads of	29.7lb (13.5kg)	79.2lb (36kg)

Camshaft:
Journal bore diameter:
- Drive end .. .. 1.1807 to 1.1817 (29.989 to 30.014)
- Intermediate drive side .. .. .. 1.8890 to 1.8900 (47.980 to 48.005)
- Centre .. .. 1.8968 to 1.8978 (48.180 to 48.205)
- Intermediate flywheel side .. .. 1.9047 to 1.9057 (48.38 to 48.405)
- Flywheel end .. .. 1.9126 to 1.9136 (48.580 to 48.605)

Camshaft journal diameter:
- Drive end .. .. 1.1789 to 1.1795 (29.944 to 29.960)
- Intermediate drive side .. .. .. 1.8872 to 1.8878 (47.935 to 47.950)
- Centre .. .. 1.8951 to 1.8957 (48.135 to 48.150)
- Intermediate flywheel side .. .. 1.9030 to 1.9035 (48.335 to 48.350)
- Flywheel end .. .. 1.9108 to 1.9114 (48.535 to 48.550)

Journal to bore clearances .. .. 0.0012 to 0.0028 (0.030 to 0.070)

Auxiliary shaft:
Journal diameter:
- Drive end .. .. 1.4013 to 1.4023 (35.593 to 35.618)
- Inside end .. .. 1.2575 to 1.2583 (31.940 to 31.960)

Journal to bearing clearance:
- Drive end .. .. 0.0018 to 0.0036 (0.046 to 0.091)
- Inside end .. .. 0.0016 to 0.0031 (0.040 to 0.080)

Oil pump:
Clearance between gears and cover .. .. 0.0008 to 0.0041 (0.020 to 0.105)
Clearance between gears and pump housing .. 0.0043 to 0.0071 (0.11 to 0.18)

Oil pressure relief valve spring:
Length under load of 11lb (5kg) 0.827 (21)
Minimum permissible load to produce above length 9.5lb (4.3kg)

FUEL SYSTEM

Carburetter types:
- European models .. .. Weber 32 DMTR 22
- USA models 1974 .. .. Weber 32 DMTRA 200
- USA models 1975-76 .. .. .. Weber 32 DATRA 1/100
- USA models 1977 onwards:
  - Standard version without air conditioning .. Weber 32 DATRA 201
  - Standard version with air conditioning .. Weber 32 DATRA 101
  - Catalytic version without air conditioning .. Weber 32 DATRA 10/200
  - Catalytic version with air conditioning .. Weber 32 DATRA 10/100

32 DMTR 22:

	Primary	Secondary
Bore ..	1.260 (32)	1.260 (32)
Main venturi ..	0.866 (22)	0.866 (22)
Main jet ..	0.043 (1.10)	0.045 (1.15)
Idle jet ..	0.020 (0.50)	0.028 (0.70)
Main air corrector	0.083 (2.10)	0.075 (1.90)
Idle air corrector ..	0.043 (1.10)	0.28 (0.70)
Accelerator pump jet	0.16 (0.40)	—
Emulsion tube type		F.30
Extra fuel device air jet ..	—	0.043 (1.10)
Extra fuel device jet ..	—	0.039 (1.00)
Partial opening of primary throttle valve (choke on) ..	0.031 to 0.034 (0.80 to 0.85)	— —
Needle valve seat		0.059 (1.50)
Float level ..		0.24 (6)

32 DMTRA 200:

	Primary	Secondary
Bore ..	1.260 (32)	1.260 (32)
Main venturi ..	0.866 (22)	0.866 (22)
Main jet ..	0.043 (1.10)	0.043 (1.10)
Idle jet ..	0.018 (0.45)	0.024 (0.60)
Main air corrector	0.079 (2.00)	0.077 (1.95)
Idle air corrector ..	0.043 (1.10)	0.28 (0.70)
Accelerator pump jet	0.020 (0.50)	—
Emulsion tube type		F.30
Extra fuel device air jet ..	—	0.027 (0.70)
Extra fuel device jet ..	—	0.033 (0.85)
Partial opening of primary throttle valve (choke on) ..	0.035 to 0.394 (0.90 to 10.00)	— —
Needle valve seat		0.059 (1.50)
Float level ..		0.24 (6)

32 DATRA 1/100:

	Primary	Secondary
Bore ..	1.260 (32)	1.260 (32)
Main venturi ..	0.866 (22)	0.866 (22)
Main jet ..	0.043 (1.10)	0.041 (1.05)
Emulsion tube type		F30
Choke calibration	77°F (25°C)	
Needle valve seat	0.059 (1.50)	
Float level ..	0.2362 to 0.3150 (7.0 ± 1.0)	

USA models from 1977:

32 DATRA 201, 101, 10/200, 10/100 .. .. As 32 DATRA 1/100

IGNITION SYSTEM

Firing order ..	1–3–4–2
Distributor:	
Type: ..	Ducellier
European models ..	S 135 B
USA models, 1974–76..	4481A
USA models, 1977 onwards ..	525047A
Static advance:	
USA models, 1974 ..	0°
All other models ..	10°
Centrifugal advance ..	28° ± 1° 30'
Contact points gap ..	0.015 to 0.017 (0.37 to 0.43)
Contact points opening angle ..	35° ± 3°
Contact points closing angle ..	55° ± 3°
Capacitor.. ..	0.22 to 0.23 microfarad

Ignition coil:
European models and 1974 USA models	Marelli BE200B or Martinetti G52S
USA models, 1975-76	Marelli BES200A or Martinetti G37SU
USA models, 1977 onwards	Martinetti G37SU

Sparking plugs:
European models	Marelli CW78LP or Champion N7Y
USA models without incorporated resistor ..	AC Delco 42XLS, Marelli CW7LP or Champion N9Y
USA models with resistor	AC Delco R42XLS, Marelli CW7LPR or Champion RN9Y
Gap	0.020 to 0.024 (0.5 to 0.6)

COOLING SYSTEM

Thermostat:
Opens at	163 to 170°F (73 to 77°C)

Electric fan:
Cuts in at..	193 to 201°F (90 to 94°C)

TRANSMISSION

Clutch:
Lining diameter	7.156 (181.5)
Clutch pedal free travel	1.0 (25)

Gearbox:

Ratios:
First	3.583:1
Second	2.235:1
Third	1.454:1
Fourth	1.042:1
Reverse	3.714:1
Final drive ratio	4.077:1

SUSPENSION

Front suspension geometry:
Caster—hub carriers	7° ± 30'
Wheel camber, laden	−1° ± 20'
	−0.157 to −0.315 (−4 to −8)
Wheel toe-in, laden	0.0787 to 0.1575 (2 to 4)

Coil springs:
Length under load of 474 ± 22lb	6.693 (170) *
Minimum load to produce length	441lb

Yellow marked springs have length above and green marked springs have length below* when loaded with 474lb*

Rear suspension geometry:
Whool camber, laden	−2° ± 20'
	−0.433 to 0.590 (−11 to −15)
Wheel toe-in, laden	0.354 to 0.433 (9 to 11)

Coil springs:
Length under load of 562 ± 22lb	7.874 (200) *
Minimum load to produce length	518lb

Yellow marked springs have length above and green marked springs have length below* when loaded with 562lb*

STEERING

Steering wheel turns	3, lock to lock
Rack travel	4.606 (117)
Turning circle	32.80ft (10m)

BRAKES

Minimum pad thickness	0.079 (2)
Minimum disc thickness..	0.354 (9)
Maximum disc run-out	0.0059 (0.15) total gauge reading 2mm from maximum diameter
Brake fluid	Fiat Special Blue Label, SAE J 1703

ELECTRICAL SYSTEM

Polarity	Negative earth
Alternator:	
European models:	
Type	Bosch G1-14V33A27
Cut in speed	1100rev/min
Maximum output	40amp
USA models, 1974-76:	
Type	FIMM A124-14V-44A Var.3
Cut-in speed	1000rev/min
Maximum output	53amp
USA models, 1975-76 with AC system and all 1977 on:	
Type	FIMM A124-14V60A Var.1
Cut-in speed	1000rev/min
Maximum output	70amp
Starter motor:	
Type	FIAT E84-0.8/12 Var.1
Nominal output	0.8kw
Armature diameter	2.140 to 2.142 (54.35 to 54.40)
Rotation	Clockwise

TIGHTENING TORQUES

Engine:	lb/ft	kgm
Flywheel to crankshaft	61.5	8.5
Connecting rod cap bolt	36	5
Crankshaft sprocket	61.5	8.5
Cylinder head bolts	69	9.5
Cylinder head nuts M12	69	9.5
Cylinder head nuts M8	14.5	2
Main bearing cap bolts	58	8
Crankshaft pulley nut	101	14
Belt tensioner nut	32.5	4.5
Manifold nuts	22	3
Oil/fuel pump driven gear bolt	61.5	8.5
Clutch to flywheel	10.8	1.5
Transmission:		
Clutch housing to engine	58	8
Gearbox selector forks	14.4	2
Final drive ring gear	50.6	7
Engine mountings:		
Rubber pad to crossmember, nut..	25.3	3.5
Crossmember, transmission end	14.4	2
Rubber pad to transmission	18	2.5
Rubber pad to crossmember bolt.. ..	10.8	1.5
Front suspension:		
* Nut—bearing to hub	101	14
Hub carrier ball joint nut	58	8
Damper upper mounting pad	7.2	1
* Brake caliper bolt	36.2	5

* Wheel stud bolt	..	..	..	..	..	50.6	7
Front control arm to body		..	..	..	29	4
* Damper to hub carrier	..	..	..	..	43.4	6
* Damper top mounting	..	..	..	..	43.4	6
* Wheel bearing ring nut	..	..	..	..	43.4	6
Bolt, strut support M8	..	..	..	..	18	2.5
Brake cylinder input M10		..	..	..	29	4
Brake connector	..	..	..	..	21.7	3

Items marked also apply on rear supension*

Rear suspension:

Cross rod to control arm	..	..	..	..	50.6	7
Hub carrier to ball joint	..	..	..	..	72.3	10
Cross ball joint sleeve nut		..	..	..	14.4	2
Control arm pivot pin nut		..	..	..	72.3	10
Rear wheel brake hose connector		..	..	14.4	2

Steering:

Steering wheel nut	..	..	..	..	36.2	5
Track rod ball joint	..	..	..	..	36	5
Steering arm ball joint	..	..	..	..	25.3	3.5
Steering column support		..	..	..	10.8	1.5

Controls:

Handbrake support bolt	..	..	..	..	10.8	1.5
Pedal assembly and steering column	..	..	..	10.8	1.5
Clutch pedal nut	..	..	..	..	10.8	1.5
Brake master cylinder	..	..	..	..	18	2.5

General:

Unless otherwise stated the following torques
apply:

Bolt size:

M6	..	..	..	..	..	7.2	1
M8	..	..	..	..	..	18	2.5
M10 × 1.25	..	..	..	..	..	36	5
M12 × 1.25	..	..	..	..	..	50.6	7

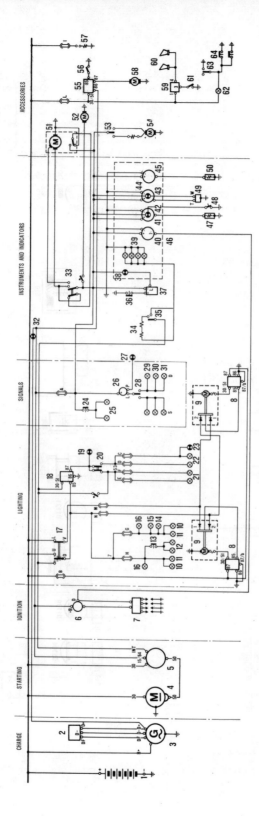

FIG 13:1   Circuit diagram, European models

Key to Fig 13:1 1 Battery 2 Voltage regulator 3 Alternator 4 Starting motor 5 Ignition switch 6 Ignition coil 7 Distributor and sparking plugs 8 Retractable headlamps control relays 9 Retractable headlamps actuators 10 Rear tail lights 11 Front side lights 12 Reversing lights 13 Reversing lights press switch 14 Optical fibre light source 15 Cigar lighter spot light 16 Number plate lights 17 Rocker switch, lighting and headlamps 18 Relay, dipswitch/headlamp flasher 19 Side and tail lights telltale 20 Dipswitch and headlamp flasher 21 Headlamp dipped beam 22 Headlamp main beam 23 Main beam telltale 24 Stop lights switch 25 Rear stop lights 26 Direction indicators flasher unit 27 Direction indicators telltale 28 Direction indicators switch 29 Front direction indicators 30 Side direction indicators 31 Rear direction indicators 32 No charge warning light 33 Screen washer and wiper switch 34 Resistor, panel lighting switch 35 Three-position rocker switch, panel lighting 36 Handbrake warning light switch 37 Handbrake warning light flasher unit 38 Handbrake warning light 39 Instrument panel lamps 40 Electronic rev. counter 41 Oil pressure gauge 42 Oil pressure warning light 43 Fuel gauge 44 Fuel reserve warning light 45 Water temperature gauge 46 Instrument panel 47 Oil pressure sender unit 48 Oil pressure warning light switch 49 Fuel gauge tank unit 50 Water temperature gauge sender unit 51 Screen wiper unit 52 Screen washer pump 53 Three-position rocker switch, blower 54 Blower two-speed motor 55 Radiator fan motor relay 56 Radiator fan motor thermostatic switch 57 Cigar lighter 58 Radiator fan motor 59 Horns relay 60 Horns 61 Horn button 62 Courtesy light 63 Courtesy light switch 64 Courtesy light door switches

118

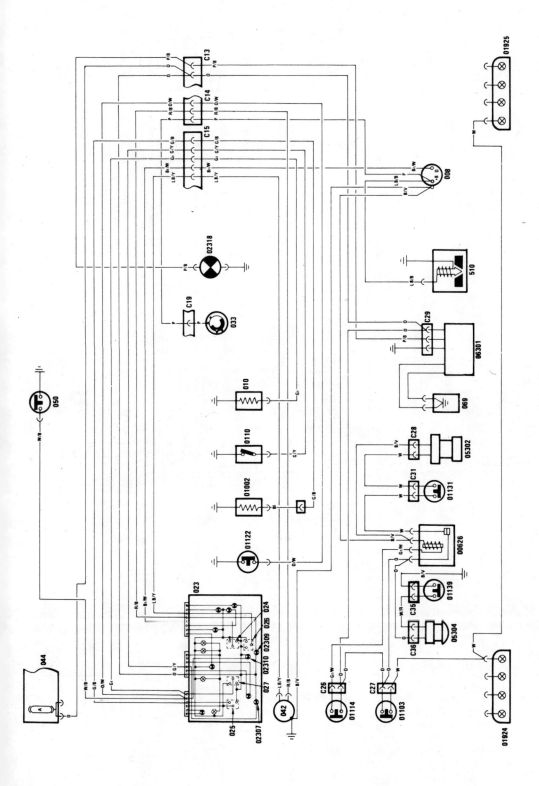

FIG 13:2 Circuit diagram, USA models. 1. Items protected by fuse A: catalytic converter control unit, diverter valve by-pass system, instruments and warning lights, distributor vacuum by-pass system

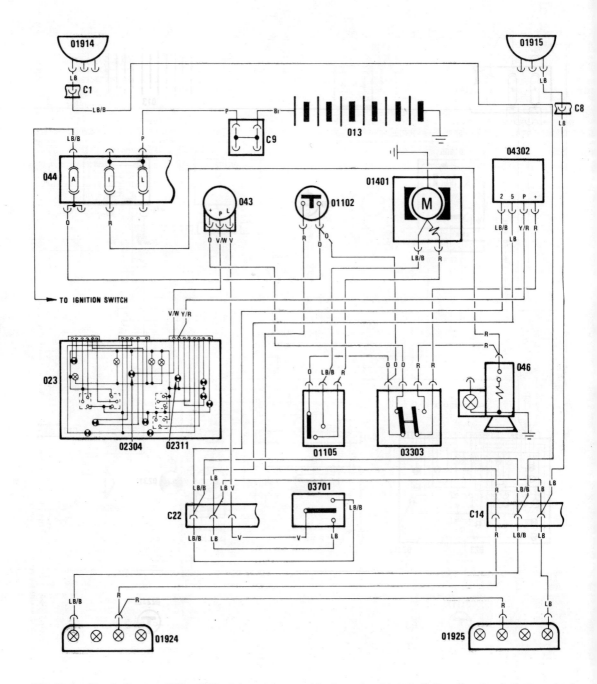

FIG 13:3   Circuit diagram, USA models, 2. Items protected by fuses A and I: stop lights, direction indicators, heater fan, cigarette lighter, hazard signals

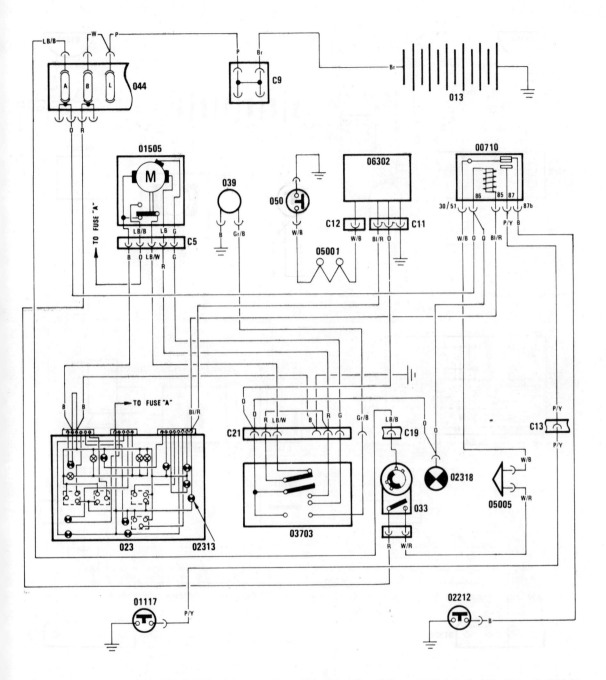

FIG 13:4 Circuit diagram, USA models, 3. Items protected by fuses A and B: seat belt interlock system, windshield washer and wipers, catalytic converter indicator, remove key system

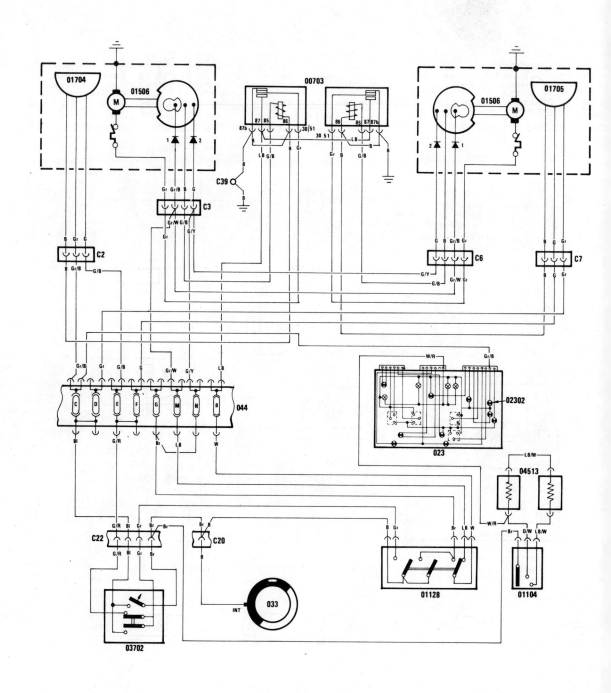

FIG 13:5 Circuit diagram, USA models, 4. Items protected by fuses B, C, D, E, F, G, M and N: headlight system

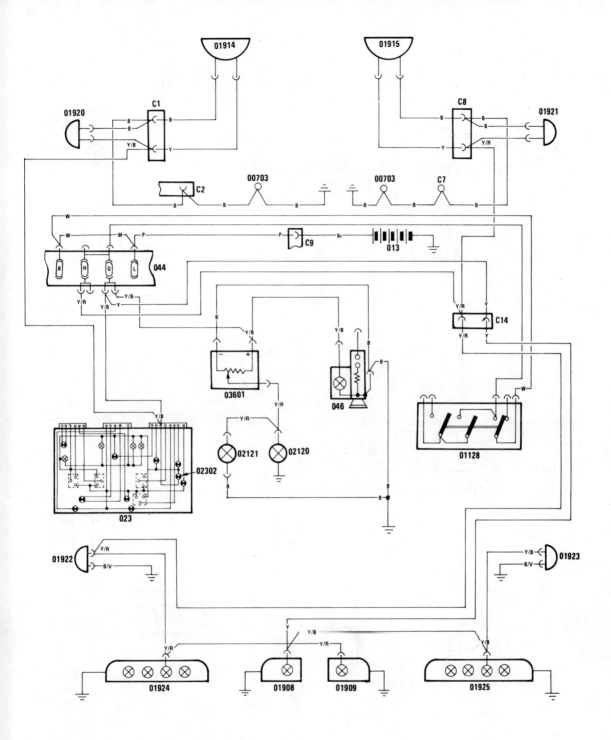

FIG 13:6 Circuit diagram, USA models, 5. Items protected by fuses G and H: external lighting

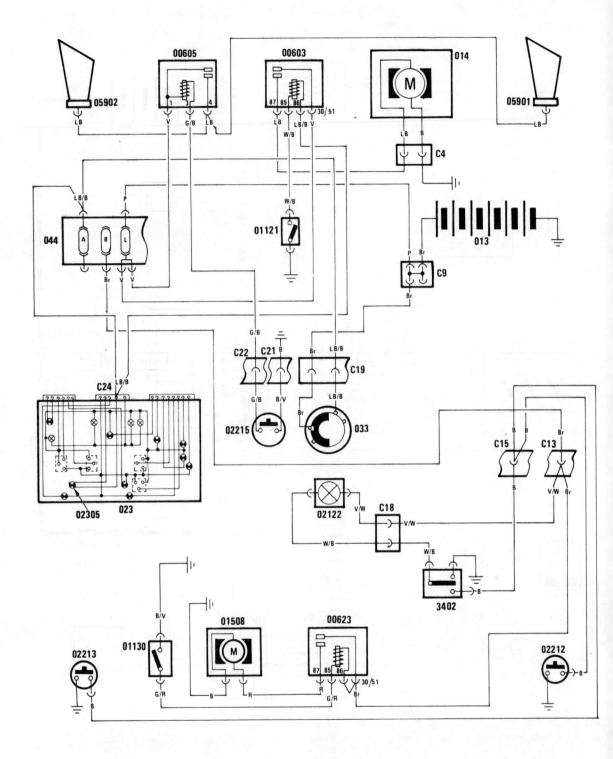

FIG 13:7   Circuit diagram, USA models, 6. Items protected by fuses B and L: carburetter cooling fan, radiator cooling fan, horns, courtesy light

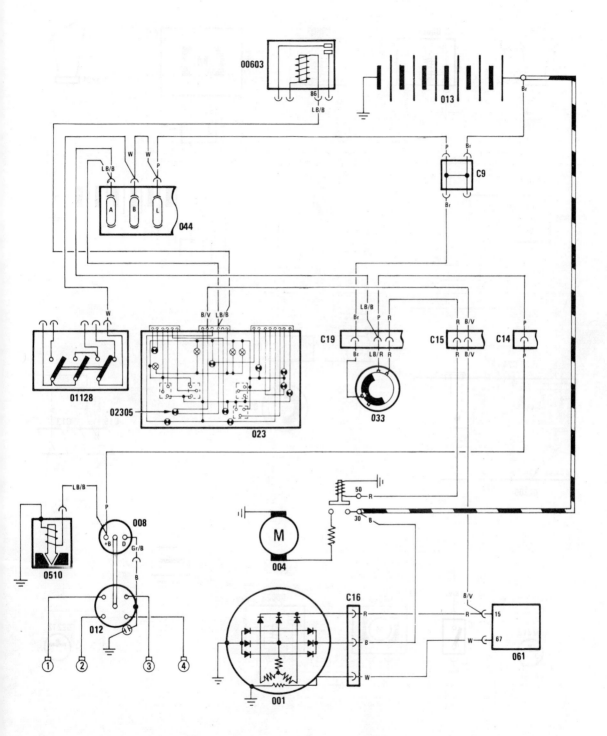

FIG 13:8 Circuit diagram, USA models, 7. Unprotected circuits, including charging, starting and ignition systems

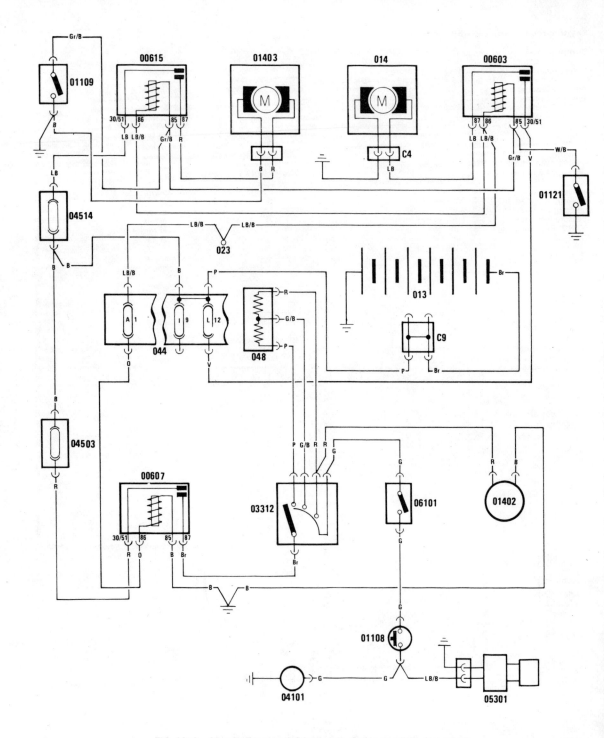

FIG 13:9   Circuit diagram, USA models, 8. Air conditioning system

Key to circuit diagrams, USA models:

Components   001 Alternator   004 Starter motor   00603 Radiator fan motor relay   00605 Horn relay   00607 Air conditioner control relay   00616 Condenser fan relay   00623 Carburetter fan motor relay   00626 Diverter valve by-pass system relay   00703 Concealed left headlights relay   00704 Concealed right headlights relay   00710 Seat belt relay   008 Ignition coil   010 Engine water temperature sending unit   01002 Oil pressure gauge sending unit   0110 Low oil pressure indicator sending unit   01102 Stop light switch   01103 Back-up light switch   01104 Instrument cluster lighting three-position switch   01105 Heater fan three-position switch   01108 Low pressure switch   01109 Condenser fan switch   01114 Diverter valve by-pass system gear engaged switch   01117 Switch on driver's belt   01121 Radiator thermostatic switch   01122 Handbrake on switch   01128 Outer lighting three-position switch   01130 Carburetter fan motor thermstatic switch   01131 Diverter valve by-pass system thermostatic switch   01139 Switch on transmission for 4th gear   012 Ignition distributor   013 Battery   014 Radiator fan motor   01401 Heater fan two-speed motor   01402 Air conditioner blower motor   01403 Condenser fan motor   01505 Windshield wiper motor   01506 Concealed headlights motors   01508 Carburetter fan motor   01704 Left high/low beam concealed headlight   01705 Right high/low beam concealed headlight   01908 Left number plate light   01909 Right number plate light   01914 Left front turn signal and parking light   01915 Right front turn signal and parking light   01920 Left side marker light   01921 Right side marker light   01922 Left rear side marker light   01923 Right rear side marker light   01924 Left tail, turn signal, back-up, and stop lights unit   01925 Right tail, turn signal, back-up, and stop lights unit   02120 Ideogram lamp   02121 Control panel light   02122 Courtesy light   02212 Courtesy light right door switch   02213 Courtesy light left door switch   02215 Horn button   023 Instrument cluster   02301 Tail light indicator   02302 High beam indicator   02304 Turn signal indicator   02305 Battery charge indicator   02307 Low oil pressure indicator   02309 Fuel reserve indicator   02310 Brake warning indicator   02311 Vehicular hazard warning indicator   02312 Rear window defroster indicator   02313 Fasten belts indicator   02318 Catalytic converter temperature warning indicator   024 Tachometer   025 Oil pressure gauge   026 Fuel gauge   027 Engine water temperature gauge   033 Steering lock ignition switch   03303 Hazard warning signal switch   03312 Air conditioner control switch   03402 Courtesy light switch   03601 Ideogram illumination dimmer   03701 Turn signal indicator switch   03702 High/low beams changeover switch   03703 Wiper/washer three-position switch   039 Windshield washer pump   04101 Compressor clutch   042 Fuel gauge sending unit   043 Turn signal flasher   04302 Hazard signal flasher   044 Fuse box   04401 3A. fuse   04402 16A. fuse   04503 Air conditioner control fuse   04513 Instrument cluster lights resistors   04514 Condenser fan fuse   046 Lighter   048 Blower resistor   050 Brake warning indicator switch   05001 Brake fluid level switch   05005 Fasten belts and remove key buzzer   0510 Idle fuel flow shut-off solenoid   05301 Fast-idle electrovalve   05302 Diverter valve by-pass system electrovalve   05304 Ignition delay cut-off electrovalve   05901 Right horn   05902 Left horn   061 Voltage regulator   06101 Air conditioner temperature switch   06301 Catalytic converter temperature control unit   06302 Seat belt indicator delay switch   069 Thermocouple for catalytic converter

Connector locations   C1, C2, C3 Left headlight motor compartment   C4 Behind radiator fan motor   C5 Under grille in front of windshield, left   C6, C7, C8 Right headlight motor compartment   C9 Inside car in front of heater   C11, C12 Right side of right foot well   C13, C14, C15 Inside car in front of heater   C16 Engine compartment, right rear   C18 Spare wheel compartment, left   C19, C20, C21, C22 Under steering column cover   C23, C24, C25 Behind instrument panel   C26, C27 Engine compartment, front centre bottom   C28 Engine compartment, left, below expansion tank   C29 Spare wheel compartment, left   C31 Engine compartment, top centre rear   C35, C36 Engine compartment, left

Wiring colour code **B** Black **Bl** Blue **Br** Brown **G** Grey **Gr** Green **LB** Light blue **O** Orange **P** Pink **R** Red **V** Violet **W** White **Y** Yellow
Where a wire has two colour codes the first indicates the main colour, the second the tracer stripe

NOTES

HINTS ON MAINTENANCE AND OVERHAUL

There are few things more rewarding than the restoration of a vehicle's original peak of efficiency and smooth performance.

The following notes are intended to help the owner to reach that state of perfection. Providing that he possesses the basic manual skills he should have no difficulty in performing most of the operations detailed in this manual. It must be stressed, however, that where recommended in the manual, highly-skilled operations ought to be entrusted to experts, who have the necessary equipment, to carry out the work satisfactorily.

Quality of workmanship:

The hazardous driving conditions on the roads to-day demand that vehicles should be as nearly perfect, mechanically, as possible. It is therefore most important that amateur work be carried out with care, bearing in mind the often inadequate working conditions, and also the inferior tools which may have to be used. It is easy to counsel perfection in all things, and we recognise that it may be setting an impossibly high standard. We do, however, suggest that every care should be taken to ensure that a vehicle is as safe to take on the road as it is humanly possible to make it.

Safe working conditions:

Even though a vehicle may be stationary, it is still potentially dangerous if certain sensible precautions are not taken when working on it while it is supported on jacks or blocks. It is indeed preferable not to use jacks alone, but to supplement them with carefully placed blocks, so that there will be plenty of support if the car rolls off the jacks during a strenuous manoeuvre. Axle stands are an excellent way of providing a rigid base which is not readily disturbed. Piles of bricks are a dangerous substitute. Be careful not to get under heavy loads on lifting tackle, the load could fall. It is preferable not to work alone when lifting an engine, or when working underneath a vehicle which is supported well off the ground. To be trapped, particularly under the vehicle, may have unpleasant results if help is not quickly forthcoming. Make some provision, however humble, to deal with fires. Always disconnect a battery if there is a likelihood of electrical shorts. These may start a fire if there is leaking fuel about. This applies particularly to leads which can carry a heavy current, like those in the starter circuit. While on the subject of electricity, we must also stress the danger of using equipment which is run off the mains and which has no earth or has faulty wiring or connections. So many workshops have damp floors, and electrical shocks are of such a nature that it is sometimes impossible to let go of a live lead or piece of equipment due to the muscular spasms which take place.

Work demanding special care:

This involves the servicing of braking, steering and suspension systems. On the road, failure of the braking system may be disastrous. Make quite sure that there can be no possibility of failure through the bursting of rusty brake pipes or rotten hoses, nor to a sudden loss of pressure due to defective seals or valves.

Problems:

The chief problems which may face an operator are:
1 External dirt.
2 Difficulty in undoing tight fixings.
3 Dismantling unfamiliar mechanisms.
4 Deciding in what respect parts are defective.
5 Confusion about the correct order for reassembly.
6 Adjusting running clearance.
7 Road testing.
8 Final tuning.

Practical suggestions to solve the problems:

1 Preliminary cleaning of large parts—engines, transmissions, steering, suspensions, etc,—should be carried out before removal from the car. Where road dirt and mud alone are present, wash clean with a high-pressure water jet, brushing to remove stubborn adhesions, and allow to drain and dry. Where oil or grease is also present, wash down with a proprietary compound (Gunk, Teepol etc,) applying with a stiff brush—an old paint brush is suitable—into all crevices. Cover the distributor and ignition coils with a polythene bag and then apply a strong water jet to clear the loosened deposits. Allow to drain and dry. The assemblies will then be sufficiently clean to remove and transfer to the bench for the next stage.

On the bench, further cleaning can be carried out, first wiping the parts as free as possible from grease with old newspaper. Avoid using rag or cotton waste which can leave clogging fibres behind. Any remaining grease can be removed with a brush dipped in paraffin. If necessary, traces of paraffin can be removed by carbon tetrachloride. Avoid using paraffin or petrol in large quantities for cleaning in enclosed areas, such as garages, on account of the high fire risk.

When all exteriors have been cleaned, and not before, dismantling can be commenced. This ensures that dirt will not enter into interiors and orifices revealed by dismantling. In the next phases, where components have to be cleaned, use carbon tetrachloride in preference to petrol and keep the containers covered except when in use. After the components have been cleaned, plug small holes with tapered hard wood plugs cut to size and blank off larger orifices with grease-proof paper and masking tape. Do not use soft wood plugs or matchsticks as they may break.

2 It is not advisable to hammer on the end of a screw thread, but if it must be done, first screw on a nut to protect the thread, and use a lead hammer. This applies particularly to the removal of tapered cotters. Nuts and bolts seem to 'grow' together, especially in exhaust systems. If penetrating oil does not work, try the judicious application of heat, but be careful of starting a fire. Asbestos sheet or cloth is useful to isolate heat.

Tight bushes or pieces of tail-pipe rusted into a silencer can be removed by splitting them with an open-ended hacksaw. Tight screws can sometimes be started by a tap from a hammer on the end of a suitable screwdriver. Many tight fittings will yield to the judicious use of a hammer, but it must be a soft-faced hammer if damage is to be avoided, use a heavy block on the opposite side to absorb shock. Any parts of the steering system which have been damaged should be renewed, as attempts to repair them may lead to cracking and subsequent failure, and steering ball joints should be disconnected using a recommended tool to prevent damage.

3   It often happens that an owner is baffled when trying to dismantle an unfamiliar piece of equipment. So many modern devices are pressed together or assembled by spinning-over flanges, that they must be sawn apart. The intention is that the whole assembly must be renewed. However, parts which appear to be in one piece to the naked eye, may reveal close-fitting joint lines when inspected with a magnifying glass, and, this may provide the necessary clue to dismantling. Lefthanded screw threads are used where rotational forces would tend to unscrew a righthanded screw thread.

Be very careful when dismantling mechanisms which may come apart suddenly. Work in an enclosed space where the parts will be contained, and drape a piece of cloth over the device if springs are likely to fly in all directions. Mark everything which might be reassembled in the wrong position, scratched symbols may be used on unstressed parts, or a sequence of tiny dots from a centre punch can be useful. Stressed parts should never be scratched or centre-popped as this may lead to cracking under working conditions. Store parts which look alike in the correct order for reassembly. Never rely upon memory to assist in the assembly of complicated mechanisms, especially when they will be dismantled for a long time, but make notes, and drawings to supplement the diagrams in the manual, and put labels on detached wires. Rust stains may indicate unlubricated wear. This can sometimes be seen round the outside edge of a bearing cup in a universal joint. Look for bright rubbing marks on parts which normally should not make heavy contact. These might prove that something is bent or running out of truth. For example, there might be bright marks on one side of a piston, at the top near the ring grooves, and others at the bottom of the skirt on the other side. This could well be the clue to a bent connecting rod. Suspected cracks can be proved by heating the component in a light oil to approximately 100°C, removing, drying off, and dusting with french chalk, if a crack is present the oil retained in the crack will stain the french chalk.

4   In determining wear, and the degree, against the permissible limits set in the manual, accurate measurement can only be achieved by the use of a micrometer. In many cases, the wear is given to the fourth place of decimals; that is in ten-thousandths of an inch. This can be read by the vernier scale on the barrel of a good micrometer. Bore diameters are more difficult to determine. If, however, the matching shaft is accurately measured, the degree of play in the bore can be felt as a guide to its suitability. In other cases, the shank of a twist drill of known diameter is a handy check.

Many methods have been devised for determining the clearance between bearing surfaces. To-day the best and simplest is by the use of Plastigage, obtainable from most garages. A thin plastic thread is laid between the two surfaces and the bearing is tightened, flattening

the thread. On removal, the width of the thread is compared with a scale supplied with the thread and the clearance is read off directly. Sometimes joint faces leak persistently, even after gasket renewal. The fault will then be traceable to distortion, dirt or burrs. Studs which are screwed into soft metal frequently raise burrs at the point of entry. A quick cure for this is to chamfer the edge of the hole in the part which fits over the stud.

5   **Always check a replacement part with the original one before it is fitted.**

If parts are not marked, and the order for reassembly is not known, a little detective work will help. Look for marks which are due to wear to see if they can be mated. Joint faces may not be identical due to manufacturing errors, and parts which overlap may be stained, giving a clue to the correct position. Most fixings leave identifying marks especially if they were painted over on assembly. It is then easier to decide whether a nut, for instance, has a plain, a spring, or a shakeproof washer under it. All running surfaces become 'bedded' together after long spells of work and tiny imperfections on one part will be found to have left corresponding marks on the other. This is particularly true of shafts and bearings and even a score on a cylinder wall will show on the piston.

6   Checking end float or rocker clearances by feeler gauge may not always give accurate results because of wear. For instance, the rocker tip which bears on a valve stem may be deeply pitted, in which case the feeler will simply be bridging a depression. Thrust washers may also wear depressions in opposing faces to make accurate measurement difficult. End float is then easier to check by using a dial gauge. It is common practice to adjust end play in bearing assemblies, like front hubs with taper rollers, by doing up the axle nut until the hub becomes stiff to turn and then backing it off a little. Do not use this method with ballbearing hubs as the assembly is often preloaded by tightening the axle nut to its fullest extent. If the splitpin hole will not line up, file the base of the nut a little.

Steering assemblies often wear in the straight-ahead position. If any part is adjusted, make sure that it remains free when moved from lock to lock. Do not be surprised if an assembly like a steering gearbox, which is known to be carefully adjusted outside the car, becomes stiff when it is bolted in place. This will be due to distortion of the case by the pull of the mounting bolts, particularly if the mounting points are not all touching together. This problem may be met in other equipment and is cured by careful attention to the alignment of mounting points.

When a spanner is stamped with a size and A/F it means that the dimension is the width between the jaws and has no connection with ANF, which is the designation for the American National Fine thread. Coarse threads like Whitworth are rarely used on cars to-day except for studs which screw into soft aluminium or cast iron. For this reason it might be found that the top end of a cylinder head stud has a fine thread and the lower end a coarse thread to screw into the cylinder block. If the car has mainly UNF threads then it is likely that any coarse threads will be UNC, which are not the same as Whitworth. Small sizes have the same number of threads in Whitworth and UNC, but in the $\frac{1}{2}$ inch size for example, there are twelve threads to the inch in the former and thirteen in the latter.

7 After a major overhaul, particularly if a great deal of work has been done on the braking, steering and suspension systems, it is advisable to approach the problem of testing with care. If the braking system has been overhauled, apply heavy pressure to the brake pedal and get a second operator to check every possible source of leakage. The brakes may work extremely well, but a leak could cause complete failure after a few miles.

Do not fit the hub caps until every wheel nut has been checked for tightness, and make sure the tyre pressures are correct. Check the levels of coolant, lubricants and hydraulic fluids. Being satisfied that all is well, take the car on the road and test the brakes at once. Check the steering and the action of the handbrake. Do all this at moderate speeds on quiet roads, and make sure there is no other vehicle behind you when you try a rapid stop.

Finally, remember that many parts settle down after a time, so check for tightness of all fixings after the car has been on the road for a hundred miles or so.

8 It is useless to tune an engine which has not reached its normal running temperature. In the same way, the tune of an engine which is stiff after a rebore will be different when the engine is again running free. Remember too, that rocker clearances on pushrod operated valve gear will change when the cylinder head nuts are tightened after an initial period of running with a new head gasket.

Trouble may not always be due to what seems the obvious cause. Ignition, carburation and mechanical condition are interdependent and spitting back through the carburetter, which might be attributed to a weak mixture, can be caused by a sticking inlet valve.

For one final hint on tuning, never adjust more than one thing at a time or it will be impossible to tell which adjustment produced the desired result.

NOTES

GLOSSARY OF TERMS

Allen key   Cranked wrench of hexagonal section for use with socket head screws.

Alternator   Electrical generator producing alternating current. Rectified to direct current for battery charging.

Ambient temperature   Surrounding atmospheric temperature.

Annulus   Used in engineering to indicate the outer ring gear of an epicyclic gear train.

Armature   The shaft carrying the windings, which rotates in the magnetic field of a generator or starter motor. That part of a solenoid or relay which is .activated by the magnetic field.

Axial   In line with, or pertaining to, an axis.

Backlash   Play in meshing gears.

Balance lever   A bar where force applied at the centre is equally divided between connections at the ends.

Banjo axle   Axle casing with large diameter housing for the crownwheel and differential.

Bendix pinion   A self-engaging and self-disengaging drive on a starter motor shaft.

Bevel pinion   A conical shaped gearwheel, designed to mesh with a similar gear with an axis usually at 90 deg. to its own.

bhp   Brake horse power, measured on a dynamometer.

bmep   Brake mean effective pressure. Average pressure on a piston during the working stroke.

Brake cylinder   Cylinder with hydraulically operated piston(s) acting on brake shoes or pad(s).

Brake regulator   Control valve fitted in hydraulic braking system which limits brake pressure to rear brakes during heavy braking to prevent rear wheel locking.

Camber   Angle at which a wheel is tilted from the vertical.

Capacitor   Modern term for an electrical condenser. Part of distributor assembly, connected across contact breaker points, acts as an interference suppressor.

Castellated   Top face of a nut, slotted across the flats, to take a locking splitpin.

Castor   Angle at which the kingpin or swivel pin is tilted when viewed from the side.

cc   Cubic centimetres. Engine capacity is arrived at by multiplying the area of the bore in sq cm by the stroke in cm by the number of cylinders.

Clevis   U-shaped forked connector used with a clevis pin, usually at handbrake connections.

Collet   A type of collar, usually split and located in a groove in a shaft, and held in place by a retainer. The arrangement used to retain the spring(s) on a valve stem in most cases.

Commutator   Rotating segmented current distributor between armature windings and brushes in generator or motor.

Compression ratio   The ratio, or quantitative relation, of the total volume (piston at bottom of stroke) to the unswept volume (piston at top of stroke) in an engine cylinder.

Condenser   See 'Capacitor'.

Core plug   Plug for blanking off a manufacturing hole in a casting.

Crownwheel   Large bevel gear in rear axle, driven by a bevel pinion attached to the propeller shaft. Sometimes called a 'ring gear'.

'C'-spanner   Like a 'C' with a handle. For use on screwed collars without flats, but with slots or holes.

Damper   Modern term for shock absorber, used in vehicle suspension systems to damp out spring oscillations.

Depression   The lowering of atmospheric pressure as in the inlet manifold and carburetter.

Dowel   Close tolerance pin, peg, tube, or bolt, which accurately locates mating parts.

Drag link   Rod connecting steering box drop arm (pitman arm) to nearest front wheel steering arm in certain types of steering systems.

Dry liner   Thinwall tube pressed into cylinder bore.

Dry sump   Lubrication system where all oil is scavenged from the sump, and returned to a separate tank.

Dynamo   See 'Generator'.

Electrode   Terminal part of an electrical component, such as the points or 'Electrodes' of a sparking plug.

Electrolyte   In lead-acid car batteries a solution of sulphuric acid and distilled water.

End float   The axial movement between associated parts, end play.

EP   Extreme pressure. In lubricants, special grades for heavily loaded bearing surfaces, such as gear teeth in a gearbox, or crownwheel and pinion in a rear axle.

Fade	Of brakes. Reduced efficiency due to overheating.
Field coils	Windings on the polepieces of motors and generators.
Fillets	Narrow finishing strips usually applied to interior bodywork.
First motion shaft	Input shaft from clutch to gearbox.
Fullflow filter	Filters in which all the oil is pumped to the engine. If the element becomes clogged, a bypass valve operates to pass unfiltered oil to the engine.
FWD	Front wheel drive.
Gear pump	Two meshing gears in a close fitting casing. Oil is carried from the inlet round the outside of both gears in the spaces between the gear teeth and casing to the outlet, the meshing gear teeth prevent oil passing back to the inlet, and the oil is forced through the outlet port.
Generator	Modern term for 'Dynamo'. When rotated produces electrical current.
Grommet	A ring of protective or sealing material. Can be used to protect pipes or leads passing through bulkheads.
Grubscrew	Fully threaded headless screw with screwdriver slot. Used for locking, or alignment purposes.
Gudgeon pin	Shaft which connects a piston to its connecting rod. Sometimes called 'wrist pin', or 'piston pin'.
Halfshaft	One of a pair transmitting drive from the differential.
Helical	In spiral form. The teeth of helical gears are cut at a spiral angle to the side faces of the gearwheel.
Hot pot	Hot area that assists vapourisation of fuel on its way to cylinders. Often provided by close contact between inlet and exhaust manifolds.
HT	High Tension. Applied to electrical current produced by the ignition coil for the sparking plugs.
Hydrometer	A device for checking specific gravity of liquids. Used to check specific gravity of electrolyte.
Hypoid bevel gears	A form of bevel gear used in the rear axle drive gears. The bevel pinion meshes below the centre line of the crownwheel, giving a lower propeller shaft line.
Idler	A device for passing on movement. A free running gear between driving and driven gears. A lever transmitting track rod movement to a side rod in steering gear.
Impeller	A centrifugal pumping element. Used in water pumps to stimulate flow.
Journals	Those parts of a shaft that are in contact with the bearings.
Kingpin	The main vertical pin which carries the front wheel spindle, and permits steering movement. May be called 'steering pin' or 'swivel pin'.
Layshaft	The shaft which carries the laygear in the gearbox. The laygear is driven by the first motion shaft and drives the third motion shaft according to the gear selected. Sometimes called the 'countershaft' or 'second motion shaft'.
lb ft	A measure of twist or torque. A pull of 10 lb at a radius of 1 ft is a torque of 10 lb ft.
lb/sq in	Pounds per square inch.
Little-end	The small, or piston end of a connecting rod. Sometimes called the 'small-end'.
LT	Low Tension. The current output from the battery.
Mandrel	Accurately manufactured bar or rod used for test or centring purposes.
Manifold	A pipe, duct, or chamber, with several branches.
Needle rollers	Bearing rollers with a length many times their diameter.
Oil bath	Reservoir which lubricates parts by immersion. In air filters, a separate oil supply for wetting a wire mesh element to hold the dust.
Oil wetted	In air filters, a wire mesh element lightly oiled to trap and hold airborne dust.
Overlap	Period during which inlet and exhaust valves are open together.
Panhard rod	Bar connected between fixed point on chassis and another on axle to control sideways movement.
Pawl	Pivoted catch which engages in the teeth of a ratchet to permit movement in one direction only.
Peg spanner	Tool with pegs, or pins, to engage in holes or slots in the part to be turned.
Pendant pedals	Pedals with levers that are pivoted at the top end.
Phillips screwdriver	A cross-point screwdriver for use with the cross-slotted heads of Phillips screws.
Pinion	A small gear, usually in relation to another gear.
Piston-type damper	Shock absorber in which damping is controlled by a piston working in a closed oil-filled cylinder.
Preloading	Preset static pressure on ball or roller bearings not due to working loads.
Radial	Radiating from a centre, like the spokes of a wheel.

Radius rod	Pivoted arm confining movement of a part to an arc of fixed radius.
Ratchet	Toothed wheel or rack which can move in one direction only, movement in the other being prevented by a pawl.
Ring gear	A gear tooth ring attached to outer periphery of flywheel. Starter pinion engages with it during starting.
Runout	Amount by which rotating part is out of true.
Semi-floating axle	Outer end of rear axle halfshaft is carried on bearing inside axle casing. Wheel hub is secured to end of shaft.
Servo	A hydraulic or pneumatic system for assisting, or, augmenting a physical effort. See 'Vacuum Servo'.
Setscrew	One which is threaded for the full length of the shank.
Shackle	A coupling link, used in the form of two parallel pins connected by side plates to secure the end of the master suspension spring and absorb the effects of deflection.
Shell bearing	Thinwalled steel shell lined with anti-friction metal. Usually semi-circular and used in pairs for main and big-end bearings.
Shock absorber	See 'Damper'.
Silentbloc	Rubber bush bonded to inner and outer metal sleeves.
Socket-head screw	Screw with hexagonal socket for an Allen key.
Solenoid	A coil of wire creating a magnetic field when electric current passes through it. Used with a soft iron core to operate contacts or a mechanical device.
Spur gear	A gear with teeth cut axially across the periphery.
Stub axle	Short axle fixed at one end only.
Tachometer	An instrument for accurate measurement of rotating speed. Usually indicates in revolutions per minute.
TDC	Top Dead Centre. The highest point reached by a piston in a cylinder, with the crank and connecting rod in line.
Thermostat	Automatic device for regulating temperature. Used in vehicle coolant systems to open a valve which restricts circulation at low temperature.
Third motion shaft	Output shaft of gearbox.
Threequarter floating axle	Outer end of rear axle halfshaft flanged and bolted to wheel hub, which runs on bearing mounted on outside of axle casing. Vehicle weight is not carried by the axle shaft.
Thrust bearing or washer	Used to reduce friction in rotating parts subject to axial loads.
Torque	Turning or twisting effort. See 'lb ft'.
Track rod	The bar(s) across the vehicle which connect the steering arms and maintain the front wheels in their correct alignment.
UJ	Universal joint. A coupling between shafts which permits angular movement.
UNF	Unified National Fine screw thread.
Vacuum servo	Device used in brake system, using difference between atmospheric pressure and inlet manifold depression to operate a piston which acts to augment brake pressure as required. See 'Servo'.
Venturi	A restriction or 'choke' in a tube, as in a carburetter, used to increase velocity to obtain a reduction in pressure.
Vernier	A sliding scale for obtaining fractional readings of the graduations of an adjacent scale.
Welch plug	A domed thin metal disc which is partially flattened to lock in a recess. Used to plug core holes in castings.
Wet liner	Removable cylinder barrel, sealed against coolant leakage, where the coolant is in direct contact with the outer surface.
Wet sump	A reservoir attached to the crankcase to hold the lubricating oil.

NOTES

INDEX